Truthful Journeys

Women's Stories of Resilience and Living Their Truths

A book for women.
Stories written by women
between the ages of 40-60 to help other women

A collaboration brought to you by
Laura Nielson and Andrea Lambert

Truthful Journeys
www.abookforwomentruth.com
Ordering Information:
For details, contact Truthfuljourneys@abookforwomentruth.com

Print ISBN: 978-1-66783-126-8
eBook ISBN: 978-1-66783-127-5

Printed in the United States of America

First Edition

DISCLAIMER

The stories and opinions in these stories have not been independently verified. Each story is the story as provided by the individual who contributed to this book. If any medical advice or information is included, it is based on that individual's experience and not by the collaborators or any other contributor to this book. Regardless of any advice provided in a story, if you are experiencing any symptoms similar to, or the same as, one of the contributing writers, please consult with your physician or medical provider before implementing any of the suggested dietary or vitamin options stated.

ANONYMOUS STATUS

Many of the women wished to remain unidentifiable, even to their fellow contributors. Although some women chose, as a part of their story, to share information that identifies them, we ask that you respect their privacy. Further, if a woman has identified herself in a story, it does not mean she knows the other contributors in this book.

Truthful Journeys

Women's Stories of
Resilience and
Living Their Truths

ACKNOWLEDGEMENTS

We want to thank the women who contributed their story to this book. This book was only possible because you were courageous and wanted to help other women by sharing your story. The process was not always easy for you, and we had many delays before it was published, but we made it! Thank you for your patience.

Thank you to Peggy Miller who helped Laura with the initial editing of the stories and providing sound advice when needed.

Thank you to our spouses…only they know the time and energy we put into making this book possible.

TABLE OF CONTENTS

INTRODUCTION

When I first contemplated the idea of this book, it was initially as a response by me, Laura, to my life experiences since I had turned forty, and how I wished I'd had a book that would help me understand what other women did when challenged with similar experiences. Primarily, I thought about my physical challenges and how I had overcome several struggles in my life where my experience could, just possibly, help someone else out there—someone who might be going through the same or similar issues or life events. After all, some of the best advice I received had come from women in the form of general conversations or when I asked them for advice.

The question was, though, how to share my experience in order to help others. Also, my experiences were just a sliver of what I knew women in my age group had to deal with. I then visualized a book with varied stories of women who "told their story." I further knew I could not pull this off on my own. So, who would embrace this concept and be able to help as a partner through the complicated steps necessary to achieve the end goal? One person kept popping up in my mind—Andrea. I know so many wonderful women, each with her own strengths, but most have other priorities that are not focused on writing, let alone writing a book. Although Andrea and I, at the time, were not close friends, we had known each other for years; she married one of my husband's best friends. I kept remembering the engaging conversations we'd had over those years. She always challenged my beliefs about the status quo and made me think about her comments long after a conversation had ended. Not too many people have that type of impression on me. She has a very impactful way of looking at you and seeing more than you want sometimes. Which, for someone like me, is intriguing. I also knew that Andrea was a personal coach, an adventurous soul, and a challenger of our typical belief systems. She lives life out loud; she embraces life, even when she is struggling. This is the best way I can describe her. Based on that, I knew in my heart that she was the partner I needed for this book to succeed.

When I approached Andrea, she loved the idea from the beginning. She did, however, have to think about what it meant from a commitment standpoint. I can appreciate that about her—she did not want to say she would do it if she wasn't fully committed to it. We both knew it was not going to be an easy task. I am so happy she agreed and is my partner, as, without her, this book might not have made it past the idea stage or have the depth it conveys with these stories. She was determined that the stories be about more than just the physical challenges; she agreed that we also encourage stories about emotional strength. We knew these stories had to convey the complexity of women. This book is a passion to help other women. Initially we spent months meeting almost weekly before we even began reaching out to contributors. We each have our strengths, and we leverage those, but we also made a pact to have fun with the process . . . and not forget why this book is important.

Andrea and I strongly believe that most of the women we know are really coming into their own after they turn forty. It seems to be a period when they are forced to look inward at themselves and not live through or for others. This is not an easy transition for some who have sacrificed so much for their kids, their family, their husbands, their careers, only to discover that some of these people and things have moved on without them or, in some circumstances, they have passed. Alternatively, these women sometimes don't want these things or people in their life anymore, or they have found a new purpose. Another aspect is those women who are fighting to keep or reconnect to loved ones through disease, struggles, or even death.

In addition, this time between forty and around sixty years old, is a period of physical change for women. Even though we all know about perimenopause and menopause, it seems as though most women don't really want to talk about it. I believe it is because of our society which makes this physical change seem like a weakness we shouldn't discuss or share. Women must still function in society, after all, and they don't want to appear weak or lacking in control of their lives. To talk about something that can, if not properly addressed, cause short-term memory loss, hot flashes, night sweats, irregular and sometimes painful menses, and more is not something to brag about, but it is a reality. This does not mean women are weak. To deal with these issues, while still trying to remain socially capable, takes an enormous amount of strength and courage. It is nothing but miraculous to watch women overcome and, for some, embrace, this period of transition—especially when they share what they have learned with other women so those women can understand the pitfalls and the beauty of this stage in life.

The contributors who have put forth their stories have done so in the hope that their stories will help other women. We both reached out to women across the United States who came from varied backgrounds, religious beliefs, and ethnicities. Our goal was to show that women are just that— women. They are beautiful, strong, resilient, and amazing just as they are. They each have their truth to tell, and each woman has a unique theme running through her story. By the time of publishing this book, these women's journeys continued (not to mention the impact of COVID on their lives), as does everyone's life and truth. For example, one woman had a second child, which was a blessing from God, while getting promoted to her dream position. Another took a trip of a lifetime and hiked various trails in Europe. Yet another lost her niece to cancer, only to have some of the last words she said after her thirtieth birthday reverberate in her head as a reminder to stay in the present moment: "My favorite cake is triple fudge. I like the cake more than the frosting."

In the end, we know that all women have a story that may help someone else understand that they can reconnect with themselves and be complete with or without others. That life is still good, even as you begin to see extra lines on your face, an extra layer of fat around your midsection, mood swings in ways you never thought you would experience, the loss of a loved one, and/or having to rebuild your life. We believe that women can look to each other for strength and acceptance without judgment. We further believe that what will happen when you read the stories is that you will find a piece of yourself, including a new perspective and some shared wisdom. You will see a recurring theme, including each woman's truth, resilience, strength, and beauty. As similar as we are as women though, our journeys are very different. Similar women, different journeys—and, in the end, a similarity that binds us all as a tribe of love and support for a healthier and happier life.

Enjoy the beautiful journeys, and we hope they help you on your journey,

Laura Nielson

MID-LIFE MATH

Me before Forty

I will soon be turning fifty, and it appears that my math teacher was right: 20 + 30 = 50. Who I am becoming at fifty is the total of my experiences and choices during my twenties and thirties. As I reflect on that algorithm, I suddenly know why I'm so exhausted: I lived an entire lifetime (or two) before I turned forty! Being ever-impatient and an overachiever, I got my midlife crisis out of the way early. I had a quarter-life crisis (or two).

The Cliff Notes version is that I grew up in a traditional Midwest minister's family and went to college to be an elementary teacher. I dutifully married my college sweetheart and followed him to Denver, where he proceeded to dump me two years later for a coworker. Not comfortable with failure, I earnestly married my rebound guy . . . who I later realized was not "the one" either. (My father reminded me that I could date someone and *not* marry him. Thanks, Dad.) I left that marriage two years after our wedding vows and ran off to trek in Nepal and find myself. Within a year, at thirty-one, I was diagnosed with a rare cervical cancer, but thanks to my brilliant doctor and surgeon, I was cured with my uterus intact. I took this as a sign to honor the messages from my body and holistically heal—body, mind, and spirit. I wanted more out of life. I quit my job as a community college professor and moved to San Diego to go to massage school because that seemed like a good idea at the time. Turns out the cancer and that decision were my greatest gifts, or I wouldn't be at the beautiful stage I am now.

The final tally from ages twenty-two to thirty-nine: sixteen homes, five careers, three weddings, two divorces, one cervical cancer and cure, rotating through more BFFs than I can count, and finally finding my happily-ever-after with hubby number three and child number one. Whew! When I hear the popular mantra "forty is the new twenty," I see it as an existential threat. It better not be because I am *not* going through all that again! Therefore, to make my math teacher proud, I stick with mathematical truths: $40 > 20$. Forty is much, much greater than twenty. In every sense.

Where I Was When I Turned Forty

On March 7, 2010, I awoke to a morning of possibilities. I was married to the love of my life, and we had a three-year-old miracle baby. Since my twenties and thirties had been so tumultuous, I was both thrilled and relieved to hit the Big 4-0.

It was different from turning thirty-nine, which had thrown me off a bit, like my twenty-ninth birthday had a decade earlier. I think the "niner" years have more pressure because they are seen as last chances. You have only 365 more days to fulfill all those dreams and fix everything that's wrong with your life. But once you finally hit the Big X-0 (whichever one it is), you know you can't cram in anything more, so you just breathe and welcome it. To me forty was like a really great New Year's Eve, full of promise and new firsts to discover.

Plus what a great excuse for a party! After three years, I had finally lost the "baby fat" and was in good shape. I bought a sleek Calvin Klein LBD to show off my newfound figure. Months before, my husband had asked what I wanted to do for my birthday, and I impulsively rattled off, "I want fabulous friends, fabulous food, fabulous wine, fabulous shoes . . . and a boat!" He looked at me quizzically, but as always, he delivered. I found myself turning forty with twenty dear friends, old and new, enjoying fine wine and tapas aboard a coworker's small yacht in San Diego harbor, as I danced joyfully in my red suede stilettos. Twenty hadn't been that good, neither was thirty. But forty? The queen has arrived. I'm ready for whatever comes next.

My Emotional Journey Post-Forty

Because of the chaos of my earlier decades, I found my forties to be a time of downshifting into comfortable cruising speed. My husband and I didn't begin our marriage until I was thirty-six, and I didn't become a mother until thirty-seven, so my forties have looked very different from those of most of my old friends. Many high school and college friends were experiencing empty nests and midlife upheavals as I was focused on marriage and motherhood. I have relished this time and these roles, but I realize that they were lonelier than they may have been if I'd had a cohort of girlfriends hitting these milestones at the same time.

I turned forty while living in Temecula, California, a small suburban city northeast of San Diego. We had moved there when our baby was six months old, where we could buy a house and start our little family. Ultimately, I hated it; despite the wineries, its conservativeness was a huge culture shock from our hippie beach town, and I never quite found my tribe. Though this contributed to my early motherhood loneliness, it turned out to be a great move to establish a solid foundation as a family, allowing me to cocoon within my little bubble as I navigated how to become a wife and mom at midlife. I never returned to work after my maternity leave, which was not something I had planned to happen. However, as I neared the end, it became obvious I wanted to be a full-time mom. I had gone through so much earlier and had worked so hard to have this little guy that I just wanted to enjoy each and every baby moment.

The flipside of that decision is that an older, more educated, and career-focused mom finds the baby bubble relentless at times. I cherished my time home with my baby, but after a year I was itching to get back into the adult world. Since life has a way of working out, and past experiences almost always circle back around, I was able to get a part-time position at the local community college teaching writing a few nights a week. This worked out perfectly as we could share childcare duties. I felt like I had it all—or at least was really good at juggling. As my child started preschool, I added another consulting job at an accrediting agency. Then as he started kindergarten, I added another side hustle writing online curriculum. The money was great, I felt busy and fulfilled . . . but I was tired of juggling. I admitted that I was ready to return to the work world full-time. My prayers were soon answered with a full-time position with the accrediting agency, working remotely, which again seemed the best of both worlds. This position—the stability, money, and flexibility—also allowed us to move back to San Diego. So at age forty, with my son starting first grade, we packed up and headed back to the beach where we belonged. I was hoping I could connect or reconnect with good friends back there in similar situations. The results have been mixed, as I'm still learning to navigate female friendships at this age and stage of life.

There are times when I am quite jealous of my forty-plus peers who have the freedom I don't, or of my mommy peers who have so much more energy than I. As I received one more old friend's child's high school graduation announcement, I thought, *No wonder I'm tired. I was supposed to have been done with the grind of mothering young children a decade ago*! However, more often, I feel grateful to be relaxing into marriage and motherhood at midlife, when our personalities start to solidify and inner wisdom is more readily available. Though a bit wearier, I have no doubt that I am a better wife and mother at forty-plus than I would have been any time earlier. For example, children will always find our buttons, but I am proud that mine are a bit more worn from past overuse, and I can turn them off at will. I find freedom in having screwed up so much prior to motherhood that I don't feel it necessary to have a "Moms Gone Wild" weekend in Vegas. (And thank God mine happened pre-Facebook, so there's no evidence for a child to find as blackmail during teen year arguments.)

As I near the end of my forties, however, I am sensing a shift. (I seem to be on a five-year cycle.) My marriage is solid (a perfectly imperfect partnership that could only be forged through our previous poor choices), my child no longer needs me as much (a sign I'm doing my job), and so the attention turns back to me—my dreams, ambitions, goals. I no longer need a job that requires me to be at home so much, so what do I really want to do? Is it possible to get back into the job market—at a level I would enjoy—at fifty? After ten years, am I able or willing to go back into an office? Am I looking for something stable to get me through retirement, or is it time to dare greatly and go after those crazy dreams? As I type these words, I have more questions than answers, but that's something else I'm more comfortable with. I don't think I am ever going to get to a point where "this is it." I think we get to the right place at the right time . . . and then it changes to a different place for a different time, both circumstantially and emotionally. I'm only now learning to be comfortable with that concept and it's rather freeing. Maybe at fifty I'll become a corporate trainer, maybe a writer, maybe go into hospitality and run a bed-and-breakfast. The possibilities are endless if I allow them to be.

My Physical Adventure Post-Forty

Though much more emotionally stable, I have definitely noticed a change in my body's resiliency, and I admit it worries me. I studied holistic health and ardently believe we are ageless, timeless beings at our core. I do not subscribe to the philosophy that once you reach a certain age, things just break down. We can be vibrant and healthy right until the end. Yet. . . .

On the one hand, since I spend so much time with younger women, I am often able to forget my age. I hated looking young as a teenager and young adult, but it is now serving me well, as most people think I am still in my thirties. I attended an event with a slightly older cohort recently and seemed to be the only one without Botox. There is so much pressure in Southern California to maintain unreasonable expectations of youth. Luckily my

Midwest sensibilities have emboldened me against most of that, and I hope to remain "au naturel" throughout midlife and old age. I think this is also a benefit of never having been defined by beauty—I was the "smart" one or maybe the "cute" one, but certainly never "beautiful." It used to hurt, but again, it is coming in handy as I can age without as much pressure.

On the other hand, I am learning that the body does have its own clock that wrinkle creams cannot adjust. I am startled to face more "minor health issues" this past year: I cannot sit for more than twenty minutes without stiffness, my eyesight is going, my ears are ringing, I pee when I sneeze, and a really mean radiologist diagnosed me with arthritis. I even had to see a doctor for hemorrhoids! Seriously?? I had two minor surgeries in one year I never thought I would need: removing a hemorrhoid and removing an arthritic bone spur on my big toe. What is happening? And more importantly, what do I need to do to get back to that concept of the ageless, timeless body?

Like many, weight has been a lifelong struggle for me, but it's definitely getting harder as I near menopause. The only skinny thing on this pear-shaped woman was my waist, so I'm admittedly distraught watching the menopause middle bulge forming. But gone are the days I wage war against my body to fit into my favorite jeans; now I must enlist its help to fight for my health. I am now fully aware that I need my body to get me through the next part of my life—and it's not a given. The first forty years? The body primarily lingered in the background, doing its work without thought, as I went about living my life. The next forty? It needs to be front and center or there's not going to be much more living. It turns out living agelessly takes a lot of effort.

In addition, I have faced another round of "female challenges." Emotionally, having a baby later in life had benefits; physically—more specifically, hormonally—it was a nightmare! I wish someone had explained postpartum and perimenopausal hormone changes to me because I almost checked myself into the psych ward as I hit them both at the same time. My moods were often wild, and my menstrual periods were progressively more brutal after the baby (or perimenopause, depending on the doctor). At forty-two, an ultrasound showed an abnormally thick uterine lining which could be cancerous. The D&C procedure came back negative, and I viewed it as another gift to pay attention to my body's message, particularly since as a mom, the stakes are higher if something goes wrong. The entire experience shook me more than I wanted to admit.

Six months after that, mortality crept in again. This time with the cruel reminder that my parents are aging quickly, and I am indeed one of the "sandwich generation," trying to take care of both children and parents. The day after putting our house on the market to move back to San Diego, I received the phone call standing in the Target beauty aisle. It was my parents' neighbor, and my dad had just collapsed. Cardiac arrest, and it didn't look good. She wanted me to talk to my mom who was falling apart. I barely remember getting out of Target—thanks to the kindness of strangers and my husband coming to get me. Hours later I was on a plane to Minnesota with no idea of what I would find. After a week in ICU, our miracle dad made a full recovery—one of only 8 percent who survive such an event outside the hospital. However, the trauma took a great toll on my mother's mental health, which had already often been tenuous. My sister and I found ourselves dealing with cardiologists and psychiatrists in the same week, learning to parent the parents. I was also trying not to miss kindergarten graduation, sell a house, find a new home, comfort a distraught child over moving, and start a new full-time job. I recently read an article in Oprah magazine entitled "The New Midlife Crisis: Why (and How) It's Hitting Gen X Women." It's filled with a lot of stories about juggling children, parents, marriages, careers, pending retirement, and unfulfilled dreams, without many red sports cars or young, hot pool boys. I have shared it with dozens of friends as we all nod in recognition. "Thank God. I thought it was just me," we whisper.

Watching those I love go through health crises has become more personal, more of a physical challenge than an emotional one, because I internalize it. Instead of sympathizing and offering help, I am secretly scheming how to avoid the same fate. My mother-in-law has Alzheimer's, as did two aunts. Off to the library to figure out how to maintain brain health. I have had six (six!) close friends fight breast cancer, and my new primary fear is that the damn disease is contagious. How do I avoid it?

And so I sit and sip my fresh ginger-turmeric-beet juice as once again, my past catches up to me. (Darn math!) A month ago, an ultrasound and hysterosonogram revealed two uterine fibroids, two uterine polyps, and an ovarian cyst to monitor—more gifts from my lady parts to return to myself. I will tackle them through both conventional medicine and natural methods, as well as paying attention to the emotional–spiritual messages. I am inspired by a quote from medical intuitive Carolyn Myss that, energetically, fibroids are "creativity that has not yet been birthed" and can grow when women "put our energy into dead-end jobs." Yup, that sounds about right. The emotional is physical and vice versa. So my next project will be determining where I want to put my energies, how to birth my creativity, who I want to be professionally, and how to integrate that into the other parts of me. 20 + 30 = 50.

What I wish I had known . . . and what my advice is to you, the reader

Overall, other than the most recent health and body concerns, I have experienced the years past forty as a huge relief—a grounding exhale after hyperventilating for so long. I had been chasing peace my whole life. During my forties I have been able to relax into an inner peace and acceptance for who I am . . . and who I am not. I have gotten pretty good at not caring about things I shouldn't care about (such as what others think of my blouse, whether my pedicure is done, what title I have at work, or if my child has the best school project), so I can spend more time caring about the things that really matter (such as whether my child is learning and growing into a kind person, how I'm serving my community, whether I'm feeling comfortable or fulfilled, and if I've had enough quality time lately with those I love). It's not automatic—I still hold my breath initially—but I'm getting better at catching myself and enjoying the exhale.

I wish I had breathed more and meditated more back in my early adulthood. I wish emotional equanimity had found me sooner. If that's even possible. I would have experienced less chaos, more joy and peace. "Chasing peace" is an ironic but apt phrase for my earlier life. There is a wise quote by peace activist A.J. Muste I now have by my bedside: *"There is no way to peace; peace is the way."* As it is out in the world, so it is within. I am getting better at trusting myself to *be* at peace, rather than *find* it.

Right before my 45th birthday, I sat down with my journal to list forty-five things that are true about me—whether I liked them or not. My twenties had been void of self-awareness, my thirties were packed with self-improvement efforts, so my forties can be the decade of self-acceptance, maybe even comfort. It is refreshing to see one's quirks in one list—the messy reality of a real woman, free to be without pretense. Perfectly imperfect. I have brought the total to the mathematically satisfying total of fifty as I head into another decade:

1. I am messy.

2. I'm rather lazy.

3. I love showtunes and dancing—though I rarely do it.

4. I'm quick to anger . . . and quick to let it go. I definitely overreact.

5. I'm quick to celebrate and be gushy. I can be very gushy to the point of insincerity, except that I really am sincere.

6. I HATE to exercise (see #2).

7. I'm a people pleaser and fear people not liking me.

8. I'm judgmental about everything and everyone—including me.

9. I LOVE snuggling and cuddling (except first thing in the morning).

10. I HATE mornings.

11. I never feel that I get enough sleep.

12. I'm constantly ten to twenty pounds overweight (no matter the number on the scale).

13. I'm terrible at taking care of plants and animals.

14. I think of myself as empathetic and caring . . . but I think I'm ultimately pretty selfish and self-centered (so I pretend not to be).

15. I'm impatient. Super impatient.

16. I drive fast.

17. I am a control freak . . . but try so very hard not to be.

18. I have a sharp wit.

19. I hate washing dishes. Really hate it.

20. I like big statement jewelry.

21. I so desperately want to be a "better person" (kinder, more active, healthier, travel more, braver, more generous, and socially active). But in the end, I probably don't or I would have already done so. (See #2.)

22. I LOVE to sing. But don't.

23. I'm surprisingly indecisive.

24. I'm almost always cold.

25. I used to pretend to be really sexually free. I was lying.

26. I like celebrating rituals and traditions, big and small. Christmas is huge in my house.

27. I'm extremely talkative.

28. Cheese is my favorite food.

29. I LOVE to cook and entertain, but it doesn't come naturally . . . then I pretend that it does.

30. I can be easily offended and worry about it for days.

31. I've always claimed to be an optimist but am actually prone to pessimism and worry.

32. I love books and reading but only nonfiction. I'm always searching for answers out there.

33. 4:00pm is the WORST time of day for me, and I can't figure out why.

34. I think I was born to be a vegetarian. But I'm not.

35. I am an unapologetic Francophile.

36. Smelling jasmine makes me smile.

37. I'm relatively confused about religion and spiritual beliefs at this point.

38. I'm a militant pacifist.

39. I'm often paralyzed by perfectionism and fear of failure. And my biggest fear is my son shares this trait.

40. I hate crowds.

41. But I LOVE Disney (happiest place on Earth)!

42. My favorite sound is a champagne cork popping. I can hear one across the room, and it makes me instantly happy.

43. I'm a bad friend. I don't really know how or in what way—and I certainly don't want to be—but I'm afraid that it's true. I can't keep long-term friends. (See #14.)

44. I talk to myself. A lot.

45. It is impossible for me to stop thinking, thinking, thinking. . . .

46. I'm inherently restless (obviously).

47. I present as an extrovert and very social, but I'm really a homebody.

48. I'm easily overwhelmed by too many choices or stimuli.

49. I'm on a continual path to self-improvement . . . but growing more convinced it's not going to work and want to stop and rest.

50. My family—my boys—are my life. So I should tell them more often.

Now that I see the laundry list, my edges seem endearing. I don't need to be afraid of them—like the monster under the bed who disappears in the light. I encourage all women to do the same: shine a bright, brilliant light onto all your "dark" places and see if it provides a more satisfying picture of who you are. We are *all* perfectly imperfect. I know this now.

I began with a math problem from my past: twenty plus thirty always equals fifty. I conclude by looking toward the future with another piece of knowledge from math class: the infinity symbol. The concept of infinity was difficult to grasp at first; it seems beyond the realm of logic and computation. But, just like addition and subtraction, it is a very real mathematical fact. And so it is with aging. It's not as simple as adding up a finite amount of years. Our lives, our bodies are truly infinite on the deepest level. This is how I intend to live the *next* forty-plus years—remembering that I am an infinite, spiritual being whose body and mind are not limited by what is behind me or in front of me. From this place of wonder, I can own my quirks, own my age, and find joy and peace in the process.

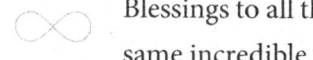 Blessings to all the women before and after who have taken this same incredible journey.

MORE THAN A MOMENT

Me before Forty

At my tenth high school reunion, I noticed that the women in our class split into different tracks. Some jump-started their families soon after graduation, while others, like me, packed up and rode the college train out of town, hoping to launch careers before we settled down. I had four years of college under my belt, but left school when I accepted the internship that launched a career that I loved in the production side of television. I had also accepted the marriage proposal of my college sweetheart.

At twenty-seven, my blossoming career took me from Ohio to Los Angeles, a year after I returned the ring. While I had gained a strong sense of who I was, professionally, he had become cynical and unsupportive of my success. Still, alone in a new city, I felt no concern about my approaching thirties or getting married. I felt certain that it would happen in its time. That was one of the greatest gifts of my engagement. The comfort of knowing I was lovable allowed me to enjoy getting to know myself before I settled into life with another.

By the time my twentieth reunion rolled around, the two tracks had rejoined. Women who had their families early were becoming empty-nesters, beginning exciting new careers. Other shifted into parenthood, and like me, took an occasional freelance job and lived happily, straggle-haired and knee-deep in the Fisher-Price life.

Where I Was at Forty

On the morning I turned forty, my big plan was to get up early, grab the video recorder, and tape a day-in-the-life of me at this milestone. I would capture a glimpse of the hectic life I shared with my husband and three kids as we navigated a typical day. I only got as far as the three-minute intro before my four-year-old decided to make pancakes in the toaster—with syrup. In the whirlwind day of hand-made cards, babysitter mix-ups, and the poorly planned party that followed, I never got back to the camera.

My life swirled in alternating currents of exhilaration and surrender. I had given up the bulk of my career, but I'd gained something just as challenging and endlessly worth the hours of sitting in the chaos of toys and homework on the dingy floor. Through the bulk of my forties, the constant uneasiness over my identity as a person, beyond that of wife, mother, and even daughter, caused me considerable stress.

My Journey Post-Forty

While my husband claimed he supported my quest for an expanded life as the children and his career grew, he still silently expected me to cook, pick up his socks, and smile all the while I prepared for bed. The hours I spent in our minivan, shuttling kids to the school were discounted. I had no time for a decompression break after the traffic-clogged commute. I was back on the wheel the moment I arrived home, cycling through homework, groceries, dinner, laundry, ad nauseum. Added to that, I became the parental caretaker. It seemed only natural that I should care for his mother before, during, and after her heart surgery, since I had proven myself amenable to family requests for assistance. This extended to my own mother as well. As her only daughter in the state, I was expected to spread the love visiting my aging mother on a bimonthly basis, until her dementia required her to move into assisted living closer to me.

Although it took me a while, I began to demand time to find a moment for myself each day to write, read, or simply walk in full strides. I was learning to manage my expectations about life beyond the family, as well. After many hours of reflection during my five-hundred-mile bimonthly commute south to see the mothers, I gained a greater respect and appreciation for the support system my husband and I had created. The last two years of my forties—and half a year after that—were the best of our marriage. Our parents were settled and mostly healthy, the kids were thriving and moving on toward college, and my husband's company was growing. Mostly, I was reacquainting myself with passion projects I had put down years earlier and was eager to resume—once the last kid got her driver's license.

Turning Fifty

I stood in the sweltering crowd atop the Eiffel Tower with my two teen-aged daughters and a plastic flute of champagne and waited for the sun to set on my forties. We had spent a full day strolling the creaking floors of Versailles Palace and its fabulous gardens. My swollen feet ached with another flare-up of plantar fasciitis. Despite the stabbing pain and the thick aromas of broiling Paris in July, I was full of wild exuberance to experience more. My husband and our eldest son were done, too exhausted and unmoved by anything but the swiftest path out of the crowds and heat. We agreed that he had more than done his job by giving me this precious fiftieth birthday gift of a rare family adventure to Paris, so I gave him a pass. They flagged a taxi back to the hotel, and my girls and I made the climb to the top. We melted into the murmuring throng atop the tower, snapped our pictures, and waited for sunset.

The growing dimness gave me a moment to look back on the last decade of my life—my struggles, my thwarted dreams, my many small victories—and I found it was good. I was happy in the most real way I knew, the true happiness that comes by way of great effort, considerable laughter, and, as usual, dirty elbows. I looked out at the gray streets below and suddenly felt like Paris in the heat. On the outside, I was a mess: limp hair plastered to my head, sweat trickling down my back. And, thanks to the bike shorts beneath my dress, at least my thighs were not rubbed raw. On the inside, however, I thrilled: for the day, for the trip with the family, for my health and good fortune, but mostly for the gift of realizing it at the moment.

I had come so far, a bit disheveled and usually about fifteen minutes late, yet I felt whole and hopeful for my future. Despite the tough climb to the top, it was the perfect way to celebrate my journey, so far.

As I look back on that birthday, marked with a beautiful trip abroad and a champagne toast to a life well-lived, I am still immensely grateful I had made that sweaty climb. Who knew that six months later everything would change?

My Emotional Journey/Adventure/Challenge after Fifty

We arrived for a week's stay in the Oahu time-share we had won in a charity auction on a rainy January day. Honolulu was calm, but the surf on North Beach was so high that red caution tape kept swimmers on shore. Eager surfers watched for the "spirit of Eddie" to sustain the giant twenty-foot waves required for the competition in the famous surfer's honor to take place. My son was back at university after the winter break, so my daughters, still in high school, brought their friend in his place.

Even before we unpacked, my eager husband grabbed my hand, and we took a walk together in the misty rain, heedless of our expectations of paradise and squelching shoes. Hand in hand, we strolled to the beach and around the resort, happily singing about piña coladas and getting caught in the rain. We arrived back soaking wet satisfied. We even got caught kissing barefoot on the porch by the neighbors. By the next morning, the weather cleared to cloudless beauty, but the rough tide remained.

We spent our week zip-lining, parasailing, jet-skiing, and paddle boarding. We found hidden waterfalls, giant sea turtles, the filming location of Jurassic Park, and the campy joy of eating pineapple ice cream on the Pineapple Express, a train that circled the Dole plantation while its catchy theme song played. My husband bought the CD and played the song every time we got in the Jeep. On Facebook, he wrote that it was "the greatest song ever" with the "magical ability to time all the events in your life." Mostly, he bought it to torture our teenagers by playing it on repeat. We enjoyed every moment of our well-earned vacation of a lifetime. Up until the morning of our last day, when we did not.

On our last full day in Hawaii, we put aside our packing to go snorkeling one last time. The surf had calmed some, but the beach was secure, behind a natural breaker of rocks. We swam and took more pictures and videos of fish, giant turtles, and the beautiful beach. We then spread our towels in the sand. The girls chose a spot near us but a little closer to the water. I placed my towel head to head with my husband's, and we warmed like cats in a sunbeam. After a while, I looked up, because I suddenly recalled something he had said, repeatedly, back when we were knee-deep in bills and diapers: "All I want to do is sleep on a beach in Hawaii."

"Sleep," I had argued, "why would you sleep when you can surf or go parasailing? You'd miss the whole reason for being in Hawaii."

"What can I say? It's my dream, my happy place."

I wanted to shake him and remind him that he was experiencing a moment he should remember. I had found that he sometimes despaired over not truly soaking up moments of importance, like a graduation or a soft, romantic interlude, because his mind was so full and busy. I had made it a marital mission to remind him, gently, to open his eyes. It seemed wrong, though, to wake a man so peacefully asleep in his self-proclaimed happy place

A few minutes later, the girls asked for smoothies from the beach Tiki bar. So I put on my bathing suit cover-up and grabbed my wallet and phone. My husband stirred.

"I think I'll go back in to find that big turtle for the honeymooners," he said after I asked him if he wanted something. "Get me a Pepsi." I don't remember what I had said, besides "Okey doke" or some other inanity. I was at the Tiki bar when I heard one of those swimming pool screams I often associated with kids and horseplay. It startled me, even though I had learned to expect such things from happy children. I made my way back to our towels, but I couldn't shake the prickle of adrenaline. I told the woman behind us that "I hate when kids scream like that. It still scares me half to death."

"I don't think it was a child."

We stood and watched a surfer paddle out to the breaker wall, but the commotion was too far for me to see. As seconds ticked down, I said to the girls, "Okay, you guys, I know I'm being mom-weird, but let's do a head count. Does anyone see Dad?" We scanned the water, and I was relieved to see him in his snorkel and mask. Until the man stood up, wearing blue shorts. My husband was wearing red.

"That's not him." My voice was calm, but my heart started pounding. I was being dramatic, as usual, writing fiction in my head. I suddenly realized what was likely happening.

My husband, a scuba diver and a Red Cross certified lifesaver, must have paddled over to help. I told the kids to wait by the towels. "Dad probably went to help. You know him." I knew, too, that my husband would be shaken up by the incident, so I started out on another of my marital missions: I would be available to soothe him, to allow my husband to recount the story as a way of releasing stress. The system had worked well, as it had years before after he had hit the leaping buck that totaled his car. He would need to talk about it. He would need me there to listen.

I trudged through the sand along the crescent beach to be ready for him. I still couldn't see what was happening, so I asked a man who was standing to watch the action.

"Is it a kid?" My heart was already half-broken for the frantic parents.

"No," he said. "It's some guy in red shorts."

My mind went blank. I tore off over sand, stones, and rocks, and then shambled up the small cliff to where the paramedic squad was working viciously, violently on the victim. The stranger, because stuff only ever happened to other people. But he was no stranger.

I'm not clear about how things happened, after that. Some kind woman wrapped me in a towel, another helped me into the ambulance. I cannot remember how the girls were informed of the accident, or who from the resort had driven them to the hospital. By the time they got there, he was gone.

My chief, immediate concern was how I should tell the kids. I felt an overwhelming guilt sweep over me: for not taking better care of him, for not protecting my children from this horribleness, for not being the one who . . . instead of their father. The maelstrom of emotion flooded me until they came in and saw the horrible truth on my face. I stepped back from the ledge of my own waning grief to help my children do the next thing. We needed to say good-bye.

They had never seen death before, and I felt like some ghoulish traitor to their innocence by showing it to them. Still, a mother's job is a brutal one at times, if done right, and so I guided them through their good-byes, holding his hand to keep him warm a moment longer. I then said mine. The only thought in my head as I kissed him a final time, I whispered into his heart: "Let me be enough. Please, my love, let me be enough."

What I Wish I Had Known

I am enough. Not because I have to be. I am because I always *was* enough. Even though I felt a step or more behind, I learned over the course of my life that so does everyone. I wish I had believed the kindness of assurance given to me by those who loved me. I wish I would have trusted myself more so I could have had more moments of confidence and clarity.

One of the great gifts of my age, life experience, and marriage is my chance to continue to hone the skill of marking significant moments, to appreciate and dwell in them in meaningful ways, so I can recall and appreciate them later. By collecting these moments—shared ones, like walking in the rain, watching midnight meteor showers in our driveway with the kids, or laughing at the absurdities of our messy life—my husband and I insured our future happiness. The moments I gathered alone are equally powerful, especially now. This gratitude cultivated over the years, by savoring and recalling our best times, became the balm I needed to heal my grief after losing him. I am grateful for the lessons this gratitude—for the good times *and* for the bad—teaches me still.

MY BODY SPOKE TO ME

Introduction

I am passionate about the idea that women share a similar story and that our compassion, empathy, love, and sisterhood are important to our journey. The idea is that we are not judging each other, but are here to support each other through life's most difficult transitions from dating to childrearing, menopause, and broken hearts and dreams. I want to be a woman that others know will be there for you, to help you through with words of wisdom, knowing that you are understood and we share this universe together. I want us to make this world a better place to be, just by be a woman that is there for other women in whatever way I can. So I can only offer what I know. And I hope that in some way I have helped.

Me before Forty

In my late twenties and early thirties, I was living in New York City, working in the hotel business making good money, partying, sleeping, and enjoying life to the fullest. When I was in my twenties, my boyfriend at the time and I drove across country from New Jersey to California to begin our lives in Carmel where there were two jobs waiting, but we wouldn't remain there for long.

By my early thirties, my boyfriend had become my husband. He was a tall, dark Cuban, and we had so much fun together. We hiked and biked and began a beautiful life in Carmel. We hiked in the most beautiful places and enjoyed the gorgeous place we were lucky to find ourselves in. We married and had two children, and I was really enjoying life as a mom; I wanted to be the best mom in the world. Also during this time, we moved often and lived in many beautiful places due to my husband's job as a hotel manager.

When I was thirty-six, my husband took me out to dinner to a beautiful restaurant, a restaurant I had always wanted to eat at. I thought for sure he was going to tell me we were moving again, but this was where he told me he didn't love me anymore and he was leaving us. I vaguely remembering being in a phone booth across from the restaurant screaming as I told my Mom. He's leaving me? He loves me . . . how can this be? He must be gay! But he was not. Susan—the women he left me for—was all girl. I became very retrospective after losing my husband. Flashbacks of my marriage reminded me of how I had really made my life then primarily about my children. I remember even saying to friends that I loved my kids more than my husband. I know now that I just didn't know how to be a good wife, because my joy came from my children. When he left, this awakening was the beginning of my becoming aware, not only of myself but of what I'd done to help create the situation. I asked myself, *What could I have done better? What could I learn from this experience?* My advice to women after this was to never forget you're a woman to your husband.

It was time to start our new life. When the children and I moved to San Diego, my oldest was five and my youngest was three. This was also the time when I received one of the most influential books of my life which was sent to me by one of the most influential men in my life. He came into my life unexpectedly in my twenties, when I was looking for an apartment to live near New York City where I had a great job. At the time, he welcomed me into his home and became my mentor. He cared about me in a way that no one ever had, and he taught me how to believe in myself. When I would wake in the morning, I would walk into the dining area and there was my bowl, spoon, cereal, and a letter from him on the most positive way to get through the day. He remained a friend for years. When I went through my divorce, he sent me *Awaken the Giant Within*, by Tony Robbins. That book taught me I can do anything I set my mind to. I had to learn how to live life being the decision maker and the only person raising my children, and the message of this book gave me courage and the belief that I could do it. I am grateful to this most beautiful friend who I did not appreciate enough. Somewhere in my early forties, when life became very busy and stressful, this friend needed me, and I was not there for him. He chose not to continue our friendship, and I am forever sad that I wasn't awake and aware. In my fifty-fifth year of life, I miss this wonderful human.

My Journey Post-Forty (Intertwined Emotion and Physical)

In my forties, let's just say I kissed about a thousand frogs. Some turned into what looked like princes and then back into frogs. I became successful in the hotel business and loved being a mom. It truly was the most important thing. The second most important thing to me was sex . I felt free, let loose during a very hormonally active time. However, I had to find the balance between taking care of my kids and taking care of myself. I got off balance from time to time. I would vacillate between being a great mother and putting on my bat cape at night and turning into a wild woman! I always knew what didn't feel good. You know what I mean, ladies, like being intimate with guys just because they were cute or you had the urge. I was on dating sites continuously, searching for Mr. Right or just a great evening. There were days I woke up not feeling good about myself, and that never felt good. I was learning when I felt my best, when I felt my most motivated and powerful, and that became an important part of my journey. I was truly in search of feeling good and understanding what that was, with the understanding of who I was in my core. I wanted to know what my values and joys were. I started to really understand that when I ate healthier, I woke up feeling good about myself. I started to really understand that when I chose not to have meaningless physical encounters, I felt better about myself. I understood that my word was important and I must be careful with what I said to people and how I said it. All of these things made me feel better about myself, which created a happier, more secure person.

It was during this period of time that my journey of who I was and what felt good got turned upside down and inside out! I fell in love—or was it deep infatuation and what looked like love? I ended up in a relationship that taught me everything I didn't want. I did know that it didn't feel right. I knew I wasn't truly happy. I knew that the anger I felt and the tears I cried were not what happiness was supposed to look like, but I wasn't paying attention. The power of physical attraction took over, and I chose to ignore what I felt deep down inside. He was incredibly handsome. He wined and dined me, bought me beautiful things, and took me on beautiful vacations. He gave me a lifestyle of luxury. We scuba dove in Tahiti, and I wore gowns out for pizza. I had a five-carat diamond on my engagement finger. I got really, really lost. The physical attraction took me down a dark hole that I had to claw myself out of with my children in tow. Terrible things happened under that roof that I wish had never happened. When I look back, I see a woman behaving like a girl who didn't know what she was doing. I was blind. I was lost in some kind of weird, manipulative love that was not love at all. I remember he told me throughout the relationship that no one would ever love me like he did. I believed him for a long time. It was how he tried to control me. I ended the relationship because of its destructive influence on me and the kids. I was confused and filled with pain, but eventually I moved on.

Throughout my forties, I continued to focus on finding a significant other, one that matched my values and was perfect for my kids too. Some of them were right for me and not for them, or right for them and not for me. I was with one man that was the coolest guy on the planet. The kids adored him. They didn't know he smoked marijuana morning, noon and night and then became homeless because of his issues. It became very clear to me that I really wanted to be in love and in a healthy, loving relationship with a stable man more than anything. This is when I started to understand what I really deserved in a relationship and what I really wanted for my life. I did online dating quite a bit in my forties. I had a few nice relationships through those years—but not the right one. I was attractive, so finding dates was very easy. This was a time of great discovery and understanding of what was really important to me. I read self-help books endlessly. I wanted to find what would make me happy. This period of my life was a very important time in my life for my self-development and self-awareness. I continued to read whatever I could that would help me understand what a healthy and happy life looks and feels like. Wayne Dyer's book *The Power of Intention* was a very influential book.

My physical wellbeing, though, was hit by the road to menopause, which arrived early during this incredibly stressful time in my life. Early forties perimenopause. I remember waking up in a soaking wet bed. Finally going to the doctor to get the medicine to stop the overwhelming hot flashes that kept me up at night. I was well on my way to the organic all-natural life-style, but I knew I needed to do something to stop the hot flashes and night sweats. The doctor prescribed Prempro, and I trusted her when she said there was not a lot of proof to the reports that Prempro could cause breast cancer. I just needed to sleep! I needed to stop the overwhelming night sweats that kept me up at night. Psychologically, I remember feeling like this is just what it is, just a passing of this age . . . and somehow you need to get through this in the most comfortable way possible. Although I'd been a health food nut throughout my life, I gladly took the pills to alleviate the side effects. Over this period of time, I got rid of all the chemicals in the products I used and eventually went off of Prempro. My symptoms went away when I made the life choice to eliminate the chemicals and eat more organic. I remember reading that parabens mimic your hormones—so out with the parabens!

It's funny though, it is said that during this time your sexual desire wavers, but mine was in full force. So when I hit full menopause, it was great. No period anymore . . . and I was off to the races! Menopause was not a diffi-cult time for me, because I took care of the symptoms and was healthy. For the most part, the physical transformation was not difficult as I know it is for some women. I flew through perimenopause and into menopause and was so happy not to have my period anymore

Even with all the life experience and knowledge I was acquiring, relationships were tough as a single mom. In my mid-forties I fell for a guy who wasn't really into kids. *Red flag, red flag*! What red flag?? I tried to separate my life, to be with him on the weekends and my kids during the week. I tried so hard to hold onto this relationship I thought was love. He was funny and smart and made me laugh. But what made me ever think I could be with a man who isn't into kids when I had two who meant the world to me? I would break up with him, and then I would miss him and bring him back. Then feel like I needed to be there for the boys and end the relationship again. That went on for about three years. That was a tough time, trying to take care of my own needs and the boys. At the end of the day, I knew their needs were more important than mine, and that very knowing gave me clarity to move on. My life lessons were becoming very clear. I began to understand that waking up in the morning and thinking back to yesterday and feeling good about my decisions became crucial to my happiness. I was clearly understanding how important it was to live in alignment with my values, and there was no question about what my values were—my children and being a great mother, not to be compromised ever again! Once I became clear on the alignment of my values, I knew this was the key to healthy self-esteem. I knew who I was, and what I knew would bring me a life of joy.

It was also during this period of my life that I finished my bachelor's degree in psychology. I'd always wanted to finish my degree but never made the time for it before. But the desire had never left me. It was simply the education I was looking for, even if it didn't bring anything beyond that. My mom told me my entire childhood, "Andrea, you have a lot of common sense; you're just not good at book learning." Those words inspired me my entire life to get an education. To further my education, I read constantly, including Wayne Dyer's *The Power of Intention* . . . well, for that matter, all of Wayne Dyer. You wonder when you are reading what will stick and what will not. I don't have an answer to that. I will tell you that the books brought me peace and a security that I was on the right path. And when I figured out I wasn't, they reminded me what the right path was or could be.

Friendships were important to me, especially new ones. The friends that were parents of my children's friends were also very important to me. They held a special place in my heart. We raised our boys together. Later on in life, I was looking for women that had accomplished great things, given back to the community, accomplished a nice lifestyle, and traveled the world. I was craving new opportunities, and they were not coming out of the existing circle of friends, as much as I loved them. For the first time in my life, I felt smart enough and equal to the worldly women I was branching out and meeting. In addition, I had been on the board of two nonprofits and continued to be successful in my career.

I met my current husband when I was forty-seven. It took me years of searching and running around with different men before I really knew what would make me happy. What was it about my husband that was in alignment with who I had become? By age forty-seven, I was able to get really clear for the first time what I deserved and wanted—for me. I was very clear about what would make me happy. All the past relationships shined a light on integrity, or lack thereof. Integrity became my measuring stick for happiness.

So along came this man who looked and sounded very different from all the others through the years. He was kind, interested, balanced, and responsible . . . and his integrity was off the chart! It truly was (and is) the most beautiful connection I had ever known. I finally was able to recognize what a great man looks like to me. As the years go by, the relationship has become stronger and deeper. He is kind and loving to my children, and my children appreciate him so very much.

During my late forties, I went on to become a life coach, specializing in self-esteem, and started my coaching business. I felt like all those years of self-discovery had filled me with a passion to help others going through transitions in their life as they related to loving oneself. I dove deeply into what loving yourself means. I began to feel great about who I was and what I had created in my life, because I understood self-esteem and the value of being in alignment with your values.

Through my late forties, I really felt like I loved the woman I had become. I felt so good about the choices I was making and the life I had created. In my fifties, the self-esteem journey came into question when growing older became a main topic. I look at the photos we took when I met my husband and say, "Wow, I was beautiful—great body." It was easy to have that look when I was young . . . so young. So this is what happens, now the tummy protrudes no matter how many miles I have walked. My skin is sagging, and the wrinkles are coming along with the gray hair. The big question at this point is, how do we love ourselves during this physically changing time? I remember my mom used to urge me to work on my upper arms, "You wait and see . . . " she would say. She was right. It's incredibly hard to keep the body we once had. I'm organic, a health nut, I work out five days a week in addition to doing yoga every morning. It is a constant struggle to keep a comfortable weight. I am cautious every day and think a few spoons of ice cream ruin everything!

Then the question becomes, after all I have experienced and learned, how does a woman become absolutely comfortable with the changing of her body? I think a few things play into it. First and foremost, my husband leads me to believe I am the most beautiful woman in the world. That helps! Second, I take care of myself. The second point, I believe, plays into how we get men to appreciate the physical part of our womanhood and the changes we experience. I know I put healthy stuff in with every meal, which makes me feel good about myself. The acceptance of wrinkles and saggy skin I have not mastered yet. With all the plastic surgery out there, and "keeping up with the Joneses," I have taken that leap. Of course, I continue to ask myself many questions about this—is it okay? What about the people who don't have the money for it? Is it fair if you don't have money, because then you look older than others? It begs the question, what about growing old gracefully?

What does growing old gracefully mean and why? Will my husband still think I'm beautiful with gray hair and sagging skin? Will I still think I'm beautiful? The last question though, is the biggest question of all for me. Will I still think I am beautiful as the years go on? How will I embrace the older years? I now find myself looking at photos when they are taken and wanting them to be taken again, expecting the young Andrea to show up on the next snapshot. It seems almost unbelievable that she has disappeared. I admit, at times I mourn the young beauty I was. The one men always looked at when she walked by.

Regardless of the questions I ask, I love the life I have created. I love that my children are doing well and my husband is wonderful. In this fifty-fifth year of life, I find myself taking better care of myself than ever before. My body and my health are important every day. I am starting to accept the woman in the mirror, but it's not easy. How can we go from beauty to wrinkles and be okay? Beauty brought attention of all kinds. I don't think I need that . . . I think it has now become a love affair with myself. How do I love the woman in the mirror every day even with more wrinkles, gray hair, and skin that sags? As fifty-five continues on, my daily mantra is to accept what is and, of course, to change the things I can and want to change.

What I wish I had known . . . and what my advice is to you, the reader

There is nothing more important than loving yourself.

1. Love should feel good, not bad.

2. Being in alignment with your values is how you love yourself.

3. Love gets you through everything—surround yourself with those who love you whenever you go through tough times.

4. Don't depend on anyone else to make you feel worthy—it comes from being proud of yourself.

Your past is not your future. You can create the life you want—no matter what your past.

ANSWERS WITHIN OUR HEARTS

Me before Forty

My children were kidnapped by their dad in 2006 when I was thirty-six. I didn't get to see them for six years. He took them to a different country, Guatemala, and didn't let me communicate with them. He kept them from me. It was crazy-making pain. In the journey of searching for answers for that situation and after fighting unsuccessfully in the American courts for three years, I decided to take a different approach: to gain a new understanding of how that situation started and why and what I could do myself that could change or transform it.

After years of being trapped in an abusive marriage, I decided it was over. I could not go one more day living with a man who was just trying to bring me down. It seemed to me that my happiness used to make him angry, and I really felt trapped like in the movie *Sleeping With the Enemy*. When I asked him for a divorce, he knew I was serious because, in our relationship, he was the one that used tell me that if I didn't follow his instructions, he would divorce me. I heard that for years, and now I was the one running out of patience, trying to escape a very controlling situation. He made rules for everything, but of course none of those applied to him.

I was working at the time as a full-time artist. My days would be connected to my paintings, almost like a meditational trance where the hours disappeared before me. The painting process helped me be in touch with myself and connected to my heart. It was like my life was a clear bucket of water, where I used to experience immense joy, gratitude, and peace. When he would intruded on that state of being, I could feel it immediately. I realized that my painting was my escape into this wonderland of full possibilities, where I was not bound by the demands of a capricious man. Between my world of paint and my two daughters, my days were filled with peace, but that peace was inevitably interrupted by him.

When I asked him for a divorce, he said he would "change," and to give him a chance. After twelve years of the same repeated patterns, you know there is no "change on the horizon." I just wanted out. I was done with the relationship. What happened next was something beyond my predictions. He took my two daughters, at the time seven and ten, back to Guatemala, our country of origin, on Father's Day. He said he was going to take them to the beach. Little did I know he had his plans laid out to go back to Guatemala.

It was a crazy time, from age thirty-six to forty. I just tried to get my daughters back. I went into a three-year litigation process. When I was thirty-nine, I moved to San Diego to go back to school to study conflict resolution in order to figure out how solve the conflict with him and try to get my daughters back. Those were years of extreme despair and sadness. I was just surviving the situation and trying to find meaning to my life. I felt I couldn't be happy without them. How could a mother be happy when her children are taken away? We had no contact. He would not let me see them or talk to them. Years passed by, and I didn't know what my girls looked like, how they were growing and becoming teenagers. He stole those years from me.

Where I Was When I Turned Forty

In 2010 I turned forty. I was back in school and, as part of my master's program in peace and justice studies with a specialization in conflict resolution, I went to India for three months to work with human rights abuses in underserved communities. I did that because I knew I needed to heal myself. I felt like helping someone else achieve human rights was a way to restore my own rights as a mom that had been violated.

During this time, I wanted to figure out how to reestablish a connection with my daughters and be back in their lives. I felt it was the weakest and lowest point in my personal life. I had not dated or had any kind of physical contact with anyone. I was emotionally isolated. I didn't have space in my heart for love and connection, as I felt that without my daughters, my life was incomplete. I felt I was not supposed to feel happiness or love without them, so I didn't. My personal life was very messed up. My children were not with me. I was on my own. I was learning to live a life away from the family that had been mine for so many years; it felt like my life was not my life anymore. I was not waking up to my children, and that was really hard.

My Emotional and Physical Journey Post-Forty

When I was forty, I lived in India for three months. I think that experience was life-transforming because I had been seeing myself as a victim of my situation of not having my children, but when I went to India, I realized my situation was very privileged compared to the atrocities and human rights abuses I witnessed, especially to women from the lower castes. In India, I stopped thinking about myself and focused on others. That was a turning point for me. It shifted the way I saw my life, and I found a peace in my heart when I was serving someone else. In other words, I was healing in the process of helping. That was a turning point. I lived out of a bag for those three months. I realized how very little I needed, how free I could be. It made me very flexible about where I could spend the night. It gave me a lot of freedom. It transformed my heart to shift my focus from myself to someone else's pain and to be of service to them.

Although it took me a long time to heal and recover from the post-traumatic stress disorder of being separated from my children, I found refuge and healing in my spiritual connection with God. I had a lot of silence in my life that gave me room for constant conversation with God. I would listen and see his signs of guidance everywhere. I felt I was being guided, and without much rationalization, I knew what I had to do. I asked him questions and found guidance. I had a little game I played with God and the Bible. I would ask him questions and then randomly open the Bible and see the answer.

Sometimes I would ask about my children, including when would they come back to live with me. The answer was: "Restrain your voice from weeping and your eyes from tears, for your work will be rewarded," declares the Lord. "They will return from the land of the enemy." Jeremiah 31:16. I would keep praying and asking over and over, and the answers were always consistent and very specific: "You will not be ashamed anymore. Your faces will no longer grow pale with fear. You will see your children living among you. I myself will give you those children. . . ." Isaiah 29:22-23. Or "I will make the family of Judah strong. I will save the tribes of Joseph. I will bring them back because I have tender love for them. It will be as if I had not sent them away. I am the Lord their God. I will help them." Zechariah 10:6. Through Bible scriptures, I received my answers. It was so powerful and random that I had no choice but to believe. The words of the Bible became living words for me. The hope they gave me transformed my thinking to the point where I had no doubt God was going to help me get my girls back. I knew He was speaking directly to me. That practice gave me intense peace and helped me develop a strong faith. I held on to that. I would go to church from time to time. I've never been a passionate churchgoer, as I find God everywhere, especially in nature. However, I remember that being a part of a women's Bible study group was key and fundamental to feel supported and loved. I remember those women who put their hands over me and prayed over me. Those prayers and support sustained me, helped me believe, gave me peace, and helped me survive.

I knew in my heart that I really needed to trust the process. There was something happening that I didn't understand, but I had to trust and know things were going to unfold in my favor. I was able to find teachers like Louise Hay and Wayne Dyer as well as Christian teachers like Joyce Mayer and Joel Osteen. Their messages spoke to my heart. I was constantly listening to their audiobooks and training my mind to think positively and hold on to hope.

It was a period of deep inquiry on how to solve my personal problems. I used to exercise excessively and almost compulsively. I felt exercise helped me gain control over my life. It gave me strength physically, and that gave me mental strength. It was really interesting that I actually felt I was in my best shape ever. I was practicing martial arts at least an hour a day, and I would also swim. Swimming made me feel vibrant, strong, healthy, and alive, plus I learned the healing properties of being "held" by water.

What are your greatest fears and how do you overcome those?

I think for me, it's been a journey to authenticity. To feel I am every year that I live, I strive to be more me, more the person I was created to be. My fear is of not achieving that potential, of living a mediocre and ordinary life, when I know there is a whole world out there of extraordinary potential. I don't want to miss out. I don't want to not feel alive and vibrant. I don't want to be stuck in a job that feels mediocre and not good enough because it provides a "sense of security." At this point I know that I don't need to know everything and have all my life figured out. My plans are just one little part of the synchronicity of events and destiny I was born with and am destined to experience. My fear is to live a life with a closed heart, with self-imposed limitations. I always love to have friends who help me see my own limitations. Having that feedback from people I trust is absolutely key for advancing from where I am to where I strive to be, open to the potential and limitless good that life has to offer.

How have you dealt with perimenopause and, if in menopause, menopause?

Not yet—still not an issue for me, and I wonder what that would be like. I have friends who have a few issues, and I have other friends who have a life completely dominated by the changes. I hope it will be an easy transition for me.

Have the changes in your body at this phase of your life impacted your marriage, your friendships, your family, your job, and/or you?

Physically, my lifestyle has changed now, at forty-seven, because I don't exercise like I once did. I love yoga, and when I go back to my daily practice of yoga, I feel vibrant and healthy, like when I did my thirty-day challenge recently, practicing yoga for thirty days straight. However, when I stop and go back to overworking fourteen hours a day, exercise is not a priority and not on my calendar. Although, I admit, even if it's scheduled, I will skip it because I think it's okay. There has been a physical change. I have gained weight but, to be realistic, I am not exercising as much as I once did. There is a correlation with my lack of activity and weight gain. For me, I know that if I go back into yoga training, I will be able to tap into the energy and vibrancy. One of my biggest issues has been my white hair. My hair turned white before I was forty, so I have been coloring my hair for years. This year, I got to a point where I was tired. I said I was going to be authentic and let my hair go white and be okay with it. Every time I saw myself in the mirror, though, I felt I was not taking care of myself. It looked a little sloppy. It felt that I was neglecting myself. That was not my intention. I wanted to find the balance of accepting the white hair and still looking hot and young. I admired women who wore their white hair with pride. I asked them how they let their white hair grow, what were the steps. I got all kinds of answers from cutting their hair really short and from there, letting it grow gray, or doing highlights to the point where the white blends with the lighter hair and it's an easy transition. I always hoped to transition into doing it. There was always a duality between being authentic and embracing where I was at forty-seven, and trying to look younger and more attractive, including looking like I was taking care of myself. So, I went back to coloring my hair. Right now, I need to look like I am taking care of myself—and coloring my hair is something I owe myself. I realize it's more authentic at this time in my life to color than to let it go white.

How did your experiences affect how you live your life now?

So, going back to a time when my children were little, even before when I was single, I would always find Bible verses that would speak to me, and I would always have them in a place I could read them easily without having to open a Bible and also pull from different authors and write things down. I created these little tools for myself, and I was always surrounded by messages that were empowering to me. Fast forward years—marriage, divorce, children taken away—and I continued to use that as a tool to go back to faith, hope, and a positive idea. I would shift my mind even when I was in the darkest place, in order to feel better. I started with Bible scriptures, and this transformed into different ideas or thoughts that were empowering to me. I knew if I read them over and over again, it would help me shift or think differently about a certain situation. One of the tools has been always trying to make words that are encouraging and inspiring a part of my daily living. Putting them in places I can see them without having to look for them. I forget and get distracted. I get trapped in the negative thinking and don't look for something positive. So if I had them in my face, I had to look . . . I used to put them on a suction cup on my shower door and read them over and over for as long as my shower lasted. When I brushed my teeth, they were on my mirror so I could read them. I would set my mind on something different than the monkey chatter in my head. This tool helped me conquer my challenges and fears. It was always something that was a mantra repeated over and over to give me peace.

What really inspires me is to be able to help people connect to uplifting ideas. What I'm doing with my business is really meaningful. I have a line of home decor products and I have designed on them positive messages and affirmations. These products communicate ideas that are empowering and uplifting—and I love that. When I was going through my hardest times, I held on to these positive ideas. They made a difference in my life that pulled me away from my negative thinking. We all have a bias for negative thinking. I sell these products, and I receive emails from customers telling me how they use them in their lives, such as taking their pillow to cancer treatments or the hospital. Or they tell me their relationship broke up and they took the affirmation to their new home. Finding that purpose in my life has been my source of inspiration that has pushed me to get through the difficulty of owning my own business and creating wellbeing for myself and others. Also, I am a role model for my daughters and embody the values that I want them to have as humans: to help others, to be of service, and to leave this earth a better place than I found it.

What I wish I had known . . . and what my advice is to you, the reader.

My advice is, don't be afraid to be alone. Don't be afraid to find silence. I know for sure that we have our answers within our hearts. It's okay to be quiet, it's okay to be still and in silence. We don't need to "do" constantly and be surrounded by people or be the coolest person on social media. We have the connection to the universe and greater knowledge. I believe it is only in those moments of silence that we can tap into this wisdom. We are so overwhelmed by the social demands of our lives. We are bombarded by social media and messages about what we need to be doing. It binds you to something. When you are silent and in communion with something bigger than yourself, God, light, energy, you can find your essence. For me, it happens during prayer, meditation and silence. We are composed of mind, body and spirit. This is your true essence.

I wish I had known that I don't have to give my power away. You have the answers and you are powerful. I grew up in a patriarchal system. Men were always in control. I learned as my worldview that that is how life works and how things are. I thought when I was married, it was okay that my husband made the decisions for the family. I didn't have a voice. Then I realized that I could not be with someone who didn't honor my voice. Your voice is as important as anyone else's. Find your voice, speak your truth, see yourself in the mirror, and find yourself. I remember the day I saw myself in the mirror and did not recognize myself. I thought, *Where is that ferocious teenager, and who* was this submissive *housewife*? You are more powerful than you can imagine, and that's your gift.

Lastly, I would say be open. Life sometimes has a greater plan for you than you can imagine. Receive every day with an open heart and be open to surrendering your ideas of what should be to the possibility of a greater life, that is so amazing that it's impossible for you to imagine.

STAND UP FOR YOURSELF

Me before Forty

I was raised believing there was nothing I couldn't do if I set my mind to it. I am first-generation and the oldest child born in the U.S. to parents born and raised in the Middle East. My sister and I were raised in a comfortable, middle-class, French- and Arabic-speaking home in Southern California. I was driven to succeed, and the path set out for me by my parents seemed to include some version of arranged dating and arranged marriage. However, to their initial dismay (though later acceptance), I had my own blueprint for my life: work hard, aim high, go to college, go to graduate school, marry a nice Jewish man, have children, and live a happy life. That was my picture in the frame. It was nonnegotiable, and failure was not in my vocabulary.

I worked hard and graduated from a top university in 1986, however what wasn't in my plan was my mother's diagnosis of breast cancer in 1987. I was twenty-two and she was fifty-two. Her diagnosis and subsequent surgeries happened so quickly that the family did not have a chance to process. After her mastectomy, she was told there was no need for follow-up treatment, and she was sent on her merry way. We were all relieved and carried on as though nothing had really happened. Hesitant, yet fully in denial, I headed to Paris for a study abroad program that had already been planned. In 1990, I went off to graduate school and earned my MBA. It was during this period of time that I met my future husband. After graduation, I followed him to another city as he got a job offer before I did. I ended up getting a job I enjoyed, however, in hindsight I did put our relationship ahead of my career.

In 1993, we were relocated to another city with my boyfriend's job and, during our car trip, I was at a gas station pay phone checking in on my mother who had been complaining of pain in her ribs. During this call, she told me her cancer had returned and was in her bones. For the next year, I flew back and forth cross-country between where I now lived with my future husband and my hometown. During one visit, my parents and sister met me at the airport and, in the car, I learned my mother's cancer had spread to her brain, that she had a terminal diagnosis, and that we were headed to the oncologist from the airport. During all of this, and in order to honor my mother's wish to dance at my wedding, I got engaged and then planned a wedding from afar in only four months, not knowing whether she would be alive to make it. We married in January of 1994, and she passed that July. I was twenty-nine and she was fifty-eight. The biggest gift was having her at my wedding and, even on that day, my husband and I knew our wedding was more for her than it was about us. On what was supposed to have been the happiest day of my life, I had a pit in my stomach knowing the wedding was really one big good-bye. The last dance was a big circle of our guests while my new husband, my parents, and I made the rounds to hug and thank everyone for having been there in support. One year later, we moved back to my hometown to be closer to family. Three years later our son was born when I was thirty-three. When I was thirty-seven, I separated from my husband. I had gone back to work part-time after being a stay-at-home mom for the first three years of my son's life. After my divorce, I became increasingly financially stable and gained confidence in my future. I reclaimed myself during this period and celebrated my fortieth birthday with my amazing family and friends, ushering in a new decade where I would take back control of my life and career in order to realize the vision of a beautiful life for my son and me.

Where I Was When I Turned Forty

I turned forty in 2005, and it felt like the world was my oyster. My sister and brother-in-law hosted a beautiful fortieth birthday party at their home, and when I look at the photos today, I am reminded of how supported I felt. I was newly divorced, dating, feeling young, attractive, and sought-after. I was launching into a new job at a large organization where, as it turned out, I would remain for the next seven years. My son was seven and, unfortunately, my ex-husband and I were not on good terms. It was a very stressful time in my personal life as I tried to balance being a devoted working mom with dating and the constant hostility in the background from my ex-husband. Our custody schedule was half-week on and half-week off, so I dated when I did not have my son. I had a busy social life and felt attractive and validated by the opposite sex for the first time in years. I truly believed I would not be single forever and was open to remarrying and to having another child so my son could have a sibling. That had been part of my original blueprint. I realized how invisible I had become to my husband during our marriage, and I was making up for lost time while also working hard to build a successful professional career.

My Emotional Journey Post-Forty

With each passing year, my career trajectory was taking off, and I built a solid professional reputation of which I was proud. However, I was working long hours and knew deep down that I did not have the emotional capacity to sustain a romantic relationship, given the demands of single motherhood and a challenging career. I weathered a broken heart more than once, dated the wrong men, and was teetering on the verge of becoming jaded even though my nature is hopeful and optimistic. So with each breakup, disappointment, and false start, I brushed myself off and refocused on what I had control over: my devotion to my son and to becoming a success in my career. Subsequently, it was clear that it would take a special, patient, and loving man to understand that my son came first. Slowly, my dream of getting remarried and having another child took a back seat to simply focusing on the blessings I already had in my life— which were many. I got used to being single and independent. I truly believed and lived the mantra that I would rather be alone than with the wrong person. My ex-husband remained a challenge, and that dynamic in the background was difficult to deal with. At the end of the day, my joy came from my pride in building a new life for my son and me, being absolutely present for him, and for realizing my potential personally and professionally.

My Physical Journey Post-Forty

My physical journey post-forty has certainly been an adventure. Haunted by my mother's passing, I dreaded entering my fifties because I associated the decade with her initial diagnosis in her early fifties and eventual death at fifty-eight. So, as I inched closer to turning fifty, I focused on wellness and being my own vigilant patient advocate. Blessed with a "guardian angel" doctor since moving back to my hometown at the age of thirty, each year I endured every possible diagnostic to screen for a breast malignancy. For years, I had undergone breast biopsies of all kinds—excisional, needle, MRI-guided—and each time, I was seized by paralyzing anxiety until I was told the scare was only a scare. Deep down, I was terrified that one day my luck would run out. So, in my mid-forties, I spoke with a genetic counselor who, after a survey phone call, assessed me as "low risk" because my mother was the first and only member of the family to have had cancer, and because my grandmother was still alive and over a hundred. I was told to keep getting screened and to enjoy my life. So I did. A few years later, however, I shared with my doctor my nagging anxiety as I crept closer to turning fifty. He suggested that I go back and get genetic counseling again because, by that point, they had more research findings. This time, I took my sister with me for support after I had procrastinated for a few months in completing a multi-page questionnaire, still feeling confident I would be reassured yet again. I knew I needed to cross this bridge once and for all for my own peace of mind. This time, upon learning that my mother was of Ashkenazi Jewish descent, the genetic counselor told me I was high risk and that insurance would cover genetic testing. I was solid in my decision to move forward with the genetic testing because I knew that I could not turn back on finding an answer now. I would be ready for whatever results would come my way. One week later, as I was leaving my office at five o'clock on a Friday, I saw my doctor's name come across my phone and I just knew. There was an urgency in his voice as he told me I came back positive for the BRCA1 genetic mutation and that I was "a ticking time bomb." He told me firmly we would not monkey around because I was at 86 percent risk for breast cancer and 44 percent risk for ovarian cancer. It was December 13, 2013, and I was forty-eight years old.

From there, a month before my forty-ninth birthday, I got on a merry-go-round of proactive surgeries to take down my high risks for breast and ovarian cancers. I first underwent a complicated oophorectomy to remove my ovaries and fallopian tubes. What should have been a straightforward laparoscopic procedure turned into an emergency C-section requiring four days of recovery in the hospital. This surgery required months of physical therapy for the complications related to the laparoscopy and C-section and, without estrogen, I was thrown into surgical menopause. Once I was strong enough to move forward with the next phase in my journey, I underwent three breast surgeries, including double mastectomies and reconstruction over the next year and a half. I have not been taking hormones and, thankfully, I have had minimal outward symptoms. I am monitored annually.

Of significance in this challenging journey, as I walked through very scary doors, my employer at the time punished me for being out for six weeks of medical leave after each of these major surgeries. So I scheduled the fourth and final surgery secretly during a holiday break so no one at work would know or be able to hold it against me. The workplace stress I had to endure was harder than the actual surgeries. My surgeons were exceptionally kind and compassionate as I frequently fell apart in their offices, due to the stress of work and how I was treated by my boss. It was clear I was in an untenable situation made worse by the fact that, as a single working mom, I could not quit, and I needed to keep moving forward and hope the situation would improve. Ultimately, I was recruited away and was able to start a new work chapter.

Since then, I have gotten used to my new curves and renovated body. Where I was flat-chested prior to my diagnosis, with multiple scars on both breasts from years of being poked and prodded in biopsies, I now had implants that felt like part of me. My original C-section scarring was corrected during a follow-up surgery, so not only am I eternally grateful for the opportunity to have been proactive but also to have had access to the best in medical care. I entered my fifties empowered—having faced my fears head on—and, by that, having rewritten my script of no longer dreading my fifties. I am empowered, confident, and have had my story met with understanding, compassion, and respect by men I have dated. I am deeply grateful for my health and the positive results from my surgeries. The line from contemporary poet Atticus, "She conquered her demons and wore her scars like wings" absolutely describes me today.

What I wish I had known . . . .and what my advice is to you, the reader

You never truly divorce your ex when you have children together and share custody. Employers can take advantage of you when they know you are a single working mother with no other source of income. Don't settle for anything less than butterflies in a relationship. Stand up for yourself, because we teach people how to treat us. Maintaining a vision, a positive attitude, and trust in the process of life has helped me get through some very tough times over the years. I am blessed!

NO MORE FEAR

Me Before Forty

Teen Years—My Life's Toughest Times and Greatest Lessons

My mother tells me I was an easy baby. I have always felt as though I was born with a happy spirit. I believe this helped me endure the severe challenges I would face during my teen years.

When I was twelve, my dad decided he wanted to move to Los Angeles to get away from the cold winters of New Jersey. The happy-go-lucky life I loved soon turned upside down. It started when my dad declared he wanted a divorce and moved out. My mom instantly went into a deep depression. With no family, friends, or support system nearby, she became paralyzed in fear. She was hospitalized and put on a lot of debilitating medication. It was scary and sad, and I felt as though I lost both my parents (even though they were both still alive). In addition, I suddenly had to become a surrogate parent to my younger brother who was only seven.

A Ride to the Beach Turns Tragic

A couple years later, three girlfriends and I made a bad choice to get a ride to the beach by sitting in the bed of a pickup truck with no seat belts. The truck spun out and flipped while going forty miles per hour. I remember being catapulted through the air and hitting the pavement. For a few moments I could not breathe.

One friend and I were taken on stretchers by Life Flight to the hospital, and the others went by ambulance. I kept asking the ER nurse about my friend. After about an hour she told me, "She didn't make it."

I awoke several hours later in the recovery room after surgery, and all I knew was my friend was gone. She was fifteen.

High school now seemed pointless. What did history or biology or math or literature matter? My friend was gone. Part of me felt gone. I went through all the emotions—shock, loss, grief, anger, sadness, and depression. I had always been very athletic and fit, but now I gained weight fast from being sedentary and unable to walk or exercise for months. I questioned the god I grew up with and the meaning of life.

The Worst Tragedy of All

Two years later, during the summer after high school graduation, my younger brother was kidnapped at gunpoint and molested. He was eleven and I was seventeen. The ache my heart felt is indescribable. I could not understand how a human being could do something like this to an innocent child. We found out six months later the perpetrator was a twenty-nine-year-old deputy sheriff with the LA police department. He shot himself when he was caught in an attempt to molest another child.

How does one recover from such a horrific experience?

At the end of my story, I will share *nine essential strategies* I believe have helped me find my way out of the darkness and into the light, and how I found my voice and my power to become a health and wellness author, speaker, and advocate for myself and for thousands of people worldwide.

Time Away and Time Out

I somehow graduated from high school with honors and was accepted to the only college I applied to, San Diego State University. Being away on my own was healing for me. I had fun and graduated in four years with a BA in journalism/advertising.

After college graduation, my best friend and I backpacked around Europe for six weeks, and I fell in love with cultures, travel, and life abroad. After returning to Los Angeles and working in magazine advertising sales, I quickly began yearning for more global adventures.

Within months, I applied and was hired by Club Med, an international company with resorts around the world. I could not believe it when I was sent a plane ticket to Ixtapa, Mexico, for a guest relations position. Every six months I moved to a different resort—from Mexico to the Bahamas to the Dominican Republic to Colorado. My husband and I met while working in Ixtapa. Six years later, we took a two-year honeymoon around the world and wrote a book together about taking "time out" for extended travel. I am also the author of an inspirational book of quotations for new graduates.

In addition to running, yoga, and working on projects that bring peace, health, and light to our world, my greatest joy has been watching our two boys grow into sweet young men.

Where I Was When I Turned Forty

Turning forty was not a big deal for me.

I felt young, fit, and happy. My husband and I had just celebrated ten years of marriage. Our children were five and three, and I loved having more *me* time while they were in school. After a few years being a full-time mom, I was thrilled to start working part-time as a grant writer for a nonprofit organization focused on youth peace-building programs. I felt great— physically, mentally, and spiritually.

My Emotional Journey after Forty

At age forty-four, I got the shock of my life.

I was completely blindsided when I was given a diagnosis of ductal carcinoma in situ (DCIS), also known as "stage zero" breast cancer. I had never heard of this before. I went in for my annual screening mammogram, but had no signs or symptoms of anything wrong. *I was the healthy one.* I could not believe the alarming cancer treatments I was told were the next step standard protocol for treating women who are given a diagnosis of this type of noninvasive "pre-cancer."

When I heard the words "mastectomy . . . or . . . lumpectomy plus seven weeks of daily radiation," I went into shock. I heard nothing more. Something felt very wrong. There is a reason we have this thing called "women's intuition."

I went home and got on the computer. Thankfully, I found information about a controversy regarding breast cancer over-detection, over-diagnosis, and over-treatment. This affirmed my intuition and led me to keep researching.

Despite a lot of pressure, the information I discovered online coupled with loving guidance and support from my holistic-minded, soul-sister friend, I felt emboldened to say *no* to all further aggressive medical treatments.

Fear, Fear --No More Fear

As strong as I felt about my decision, the grim cancer recurrence statistics, thoughts of cancer spreading, and fears of dying early from breast cancer would creep in.

What helped me most to overcome the worry and "what ifs"?

I have always been a seeker of truth. From a young age, I devoured books in search of answers to life's deepest questions. I chose journalism as my major in college. I now felt driven with a fierce passion as if I was an investigative journalist.

Over the next two years, I collected science-based studies, resources, and expert statements in support of "less is more," especially for low-risk DCIS. Sadly much of the wisdom I was finding was not being publicized. Women continued to be frightened and pressured into aggressive treatments. The studies and articles I found were often overshadowed by mainstream media hype and a culture of fear around breast cancer, despite conclusive evidence of massive over-diagnosis and over-treatment.

I was amazed to learn that over-diagnosis of breast cancer was potentially affecting over fifty thousand healthy women every year in the United States alone—and ten thousand more worldwide. Many of these women might not even realize they were very likely subjected to harm rather than life-saving benefits of "early detection." The problem was often down-played in the medical literature as an "unforeseen consequence" of screening mammography.

Having been traumatized emotionally as well as physically with multiple "blind" surgeries that left positive or close margins (and the need for more surgery), not to mention their ongoing worries and medical bills, I felt women in the general public, especially women in their forties, needed to be forewarned.

I was also surprised that there was absolutely no organized support group or resources for women diagnosed with pure DCIS. When I inquired of my health-care provider about a DCIS-specific support group, I was told they did not have one. I called every medical institution in San Diego and all said the same thing. There was no DCIS-specific support group, but I could attend a breast cancer support group.

I decided to check out one of the local breast cancer support group meetings. I knew right away I would never go back. It was anything but the support I was looking for. I wanted to connect with like-minded women on a more holistic lifestyle approach to reduce risk of a future breast cancer. I was so sad to hear all the stories about mastectomies, lumpectomies, radiation therapy, chemo, and other drug side effects.

For me, this was the complete opposite of the kind of support I was looking for. Online forums were no better. There was a lot of fear-mongering and criticism for even bringing up questions, studies, articles, and experts discussing the "less is more" approach to DCIS. I felt very alone.

It was almost as if I was being discriminated against because I chose not to partake of standard-of-care treatments. I knew in my heart that there had to be other women in the world who felt just like me.

Being the Change

Gandhi said, "We must be the change we wish to see in the world." After nearly two years of research and feeling bullied and silenced by women in online forums, I decided I would create exactly what I was looking for but had never found.

With no knowledge whatsoever of how to create a website, I was determined to learn. I watched YouTube videos and tutorials on "How to create a WordPress website."

DCIS 411 was birthed in less than one month. *"Support. Options. Sanity."* was the tagline I chose.

I was so thrilled to have a way to share my two-year emotional rollercoaster journey and research. It was as though a force was fueling me to work on my website night and day. I felt compelled to help women worldwide access critical information that could support them in understanding their diagnosis better before rushing into potentially damaging, irreversible, and often unnecessary "cancer" treatments.

It was important for me to ensure this website was an inclusive space where women could feel safe to share their questions and concerns and connect with others going through similar experiences. I truly feel this website is instrumental in filling a missing gap in women's health-care today.

Through my personal experience with "stage zero" breast cancer, I went through an incredible life transformation. I was blessed to come to a new understanding about cancer (and all illness) and how the body heals and thrives. I went from being frightened, confused, and anxious to feeling calm, empowered, and inspired. I became an avid researcher, blogger, and advocate for informed decision-making and proactive wellness practices.

Since 2011, this simple amateur website has positively impacted thousands of women's lives around the world. I continue to feel compelled to share the resources and wisdom I discover—and to encourage women to be informed and empowered in their journeys to health, wellness, and peace of mind.

Finding My Calling

Having a "cancer scare" brought me to a deeper level of purpose. At age forty-five, my calling became crystal clear. I started living, learning, and sharing my path via my website and social media. More and more women and their loved ones contacted me in a state of overwhelm, confusion, and fear. I was happy to be a source of support, guidance, and solace. I made it a priority to be available to anyone who contacted me via text, email, Facebook, and phone. I loved helping people find a sense of peace and empowerment, no matter what treatment and lifestyle decisions they made.

Shifting Focus to "Food as Medicine"

Along with intensive research about DCIS, I was equally fascinated with food as medicine. I watched YouTube videos and read books and articles nonstop. In 2013, at age forty-eight, I enrolled in a program to become a certified nutritionist consultant.

Soon after receiving my certification, I was hired to create a nutrition education program for a nonprofit organization serving low-income children.

At age fifty, I continued to learn. I completed an instructor training program for a nationally acclaimed "Natural Healing and Cooking Program."

Paying It Forward

After working and volunteering for nonprofit organizations for over ten years, I had many ideas and visions for creating my own nonprofit. I wanted to combine all I had learned about food and lifestyle into a program that would serve people who were facing cancer or other serious life or health challenges.

Once again, I researched nonstop. I was thrilled to find a fiscal sponsor, which helped me bring my vision of a nonprofit organization to fruition without all the hassle and red tape.

At age fifty-one, Give Wellness was birthed. The mission of Give Wellness is to pay *wellness* forward by collaborating with like-minded organizations in support of educational programs and wellness scholarships.

A New Career Emerges—Patient Advocacy

Just as I launched Give Wellness, I was recruited as a patient advocate consultant on two multimillion-dollar national and international cancer research projects led by some of the world's top breast cancer experts. The goal of this research is to study less aggressive treatment options and reduce over-treatment. It is extremely fulfilling to have DCIS 411 recognized as a partner organization and to be able to represent patient perspectives, which is highly valued within these projects.

Serendipity and Synchronicity—Magic Happens

Albert Einstein said, "There are only two ways to live your life. One is as though nothing is a miracle. The other is as though everything is a miracle."

When you are "in the zone" of your heart and soul, serendipity and synchronicity happen.

I kept experiencing this magic. The puzzle pieces (lessons, relationships, teachers, angels, wisdom, experience, skills, money, friends, job opportunities) appeared as needed—when I was truly ready for each one.

As Oprah said, "I believe luck is preparation meeting opportunity. If you hadn't been prepared when the opportunity came along, you wouldn't have been lucky."

The best preparation is staying true to your soul. It may be endless hours of dedication, but it won't really feel like work. It will feel organic and effortless. There is no need to force anything quickly or convince anyone. Cheerleaders appear and naysayers fall away when you are in the "magic" zone.

My Physical Adventure Post-Forty

With a "stage zero" breast cancer diagnosis, I was encouraged by doctors to take an anti-hormone drug called tamoxifen daily for five years as a way to block estrogen to potentially "prevent" breast cancer.

With instant menopause and a ton of other side effects including endometrial cancer: "no way" was my response to the doctors about tamoxifen.

What about bioidentical hormones? Was this safe? Were any of the testing methodologies even reliable?

Again, I researched like crazy. I also consulted with a gynecologist, a naturopathic doctor, and an integrative doctor. I did saliva, blood, and urine tests. I got different results from different tests. I wasn't convinced any of it was reliable. I ended up trying bioidentical hormones for a short period, but stopped since I didn't really have any significant symptoms that justified the unknown downsides or risks.

It was not until around age forty-eight that I started getting more noticeable perimenopausal symptoms. I decided, after all my research, the best way to deal with balancing hormones was . . . naturally. This included a super healthy whole-food plant-based diet, daily exercise, yoga, quality sleep, and minimizing environmental toxins, chemicals, stress, and toxic relationships.

It's been over eight years on this journey of living and sharing optimal wellness. My holistic approach is summed up on a one-page Breast Wellness Checklist which is posted on DCIS 411. This document answers all the questions about what to eat and what to avoid as well as what women really need to know about screening options.

A few book recommendations about Managing Midlife Hormones and Menopause:

- *Goddesses Never Age* and *The Wisdom of Menopause* by Christiane Northrup, MD

- *Medical Medium: Thyroid Healing* by Anthony William

- *Food Over Medicine: The Conversation That Could Save Your Life* by Pam Popper, PhD, ND

What I wish I had known . . . and what my advice is to you, the reader

Nine Ways to Find Health and Happiness after Forty

Below are a few things I feel that I believe are essential:

1. **Be an educated and empowered health-care consumer**

I wish I had been more informed and empowered when it came to health and especially breast cancer screening and so-called "early detection." I had no idea about the potential harm of mammograms, especially for women in their forties. I had to learn the hard way about the problem of over-diagnosis and how this can turn a healthy woman's life completely upside

58

down. My advice to women is to understand both the pros and cons of any medical tests, procedures, or drugs.

I have found a simple way to be more empowered and get alternative perspectives on health issues, screening tests, drugs, and the like is by utilizing searches such as:

- "Pros and cons of _____ .

- "Natural remedies for _____.

I also wish I had known about "food as medicine." Being a vegetarian for many years, I thought I was really healthy. Having later studied and read many books on nutrition throughout my forties, I realized I knew very little about high-quality nutrition.

My advice is to stay away from fad diets and processed foods. For the last eight years, I have followed a whole-food plant-based diet and lifestyle. I am convinced this is the best way to avoid and heal disease. I think of healthy, delicious food from nature as a gift to my body, mind, and spirit. Keep it simple. Recite this mantra: "My body is a temple. I allow only the highest, healthiest, purest to enter."

2. Exercise

I was in a really bad car accident when I was fifteen, and one of my best friends died. I was unable to walk for several months, and I gained weight quickly. I felt sad, angry, confused, disconnected, fat, and depressed.

There is no way I could have regained my physical, emotional, and spiritual well-being without exercise. I started jogging one mile around the high school track, then two, then three. In college, I increased to four miles daily. I have rarely missed a day of running since. I am so totally convinced of the benefits of exercise that I plan when I will run or go to the gym each day. Listening to uplifting music is an added bonus.

I recommend making exercise a priority and a daily ritual. Swim, dance, walk—do what you can.

3. Spiritual wisdom

I started collecting positive affirmations, poems, quotes, and lyrics after my friend died at fifteen. I also started reading "spiritual" books at the same time. I still try to read or listen to something of a spiritual nature every day. This has brought me my greatest insights, new perspectives, hope, inspiration, motivation, empowerment, upliftment, peace, lightness, and joy. (See books I recommend at the end of my story).

4. Connection

Women need women. Support, compassion, empathy, understanding, and connection are critical to health and happiness as we go through trials and tribulations.

I joined a weekly "moms group" when my kids were little. A few of these women have remained my best friends. In my forties, I was invited to another group called "Like-Minded Women." Many of these women have become dear friends and often infuse new inspiration into my life. Whether I need a prayer or a laugh, I know I have a few true-blue friends I can share anything with.

Online groups can also be a source of connection and ongoing learning. Sometimes family, friends, even a therapist won't understand as well as those going through a similar life challenge.

A friend encouraged me to start a Facebook group called "Donna's Choice: Global Healing from the Inside Out." Here is the description:

Inspired by Donna Pinto's choice to take the path of natural, integrative health and healing over "standard of care" Western medical treatments, we gather together to support all of us in discovering and living a life of health and happiness. This is an open forum to share wise eating habits, natural remedies and the embrace of principles of personal empowerment and enlightenment.

5. Yoga and Deep Relaxation

Yoga impacted my life in a profound way when I was introduced to an extraordinary yoga and meditation teacher from India. I wrote a blog post called Peace, Love & "The Science of Happiness" about yoga and my teacher, Kay:

I got hooked on Kay's hatha yoga class ten years ago. I remember how her teachings brought such peace and calm to me immediately following 9-11 when terror and fear permeated our society. I was a new mom with typical anxieties, and my mind couldn't rest. Kay changed all that for me. After an hour and a half of yoga postures where Kay gave detailed descriptions of the internal workout of organs intertwined with ancient wisdom from the yogis, Kay guided me into a deep relaxation which can only be described as "bliss." According to Kay, yoga is "the science of happiness." And I am a true believer!

I recommend finding a yoga teacher you resonate with and stick with it. It is a direct path to mind–body–spirit wisdom and wellness.

6. Keep Following Your Heart and Inner Guidance System (IGS)

My intuition spoke to me when faced with a DCIS diagnosis. This led me to a total life transformation and finding my "calling" at age forty-five. I feel we are all blessed with this amazing built-in guidance system.

7. Gratitude

Gratitude can literally change our vibration. All it takes is focusing on what we have . . . from oxygen to a bed to a toilet. There is always something to be grateful for.

8. Detach with Love

This is probably one of the toughest lessons people who are naturally caring and empathetic need to learn.

9. *Travel Light. Live Light. Spread the Light. Be the Light.*

My motto—I found it on a tea bag.

I am forever grateful for the wisdom I attained from the following books which I highly recommend:

Illusions by Richard Bach; *Many Lives, Many Masters* by Dr. Brian Weiss; *The Way of the Peaceful Warrior* by Dan Millman; *Man's Search for Meaning* by Victor Frankl; *The Awakening of Intelligence* by Krishnamurti; *Love* by Leo Buscaglia; *Siddhartha* by Herman Hesse; *Seat of the Soul* by Gary Zukav; *The Tao of Pooh* by Benjamin Hoff; *Out on a Limb* by Shirley MacLaine; *Autobiography of a Yogi* by Paramahansa Yogananda; *I Am That* by Sri Nisargadatta Maharaj; *The Prophet* by Kahlil Gibran; *The Power of Now* by Eckhart Tolle; *The Power of Intention* by Dr. Wayne Dyer; *A Return to Love: Reflections on the Principle of A Course in Miracles* by Marianne Williamson; *Power vs. Force* by Dr. David Hawkins; *Ask and It Is Given* by Esther and Jerry Hicks

This author chose not to be anonymous and to disclose her name and identifiable resources.

FINDING MY OWN HAPPINESS

Me before Forty

If I had to sum up my life before forty, I would say that it was full of challenges, some normal, some not so normal; however, I wouldn't change a thing. Those challenges made me the person I am today, and I'm happy to say, I like that person. On the normal side, my parents divorced when I was very young. I was married, divorced and remarried by the time I was thirty. I moved cross country three times due to job relocations and was saddled with the normal financial stress of trying to pay a mortgage and establish myself early in life. Some challenges, however, were a bit more intense. I terminated my relationship with my mother due to a history of unsafe decisions on her part. I watched my father struggle with alcohol for many years and played a large role in his recovery. I had a pretty significant cancer scare in my teens that lingered well into my forties. I had a series of miscarriages and pregnancy challenges ultimately ending with my son being stillborn in my seventh month of pregnancy. I then adopted two children from Russia, one of whom had some pretty significant special needs.

I also had some amazing experiences as well; I traveled a lot, had a relatively happy marriage, earned both my bachelor's and master's degrees on my own dime while working full time. I established myself in my career, started a family even though it was difficult, and found a great support system of friends and family. I settled into my new West Coast home and learned a tremendous amount about myself throughout each part of the journey.

Where I Was When I Turned Forty

When I turned forty, I was in the best physical shape of my life and was feeling healthy and strong. I bought into the whole "forty is the new thirty" mindset and really didn't let the age change bother me at all. I was working out daily, training like an athlete, and feeling like I could tackle the world. I was struggling a little with the day-to-day stress of having two young children and getting my special-needs son the help he needed. Financially, we were doing fine although I was always concerned that we spent more than we should. We were in an expensive part of the country where people often live beyond their means, and we were no exception. Looking back, I think turning forty was pretty boring and uneventful for me, but that changed quickly.

My Emotional Journey Post-Forty

Shortly after my fortieth birthday, I stopped working full time in order to focus on my son's care. Financially, my husband could handle things, but we did not do a good job reducing our spending to adjust to our new income level. I continued to exercise as a primary stress reliever and probably even ramped it up more. As a result, it wasn't long before I started getting a lot of outside attention from both men and women. Women would ask me for advice or look to me for inspiration, and I was getting hit on by men twenty years younger than me. I honestly started to feel attractive for the first time in my life. This newfound attention made me realize that I was very sexually unfulfilled, not just in my current marriage, but perhaps in every relationship before that. My husband and I were best friends, and we went through many things together that I couldn't imagine going through with anyone else. However, the relationship was never a strong physical one, and I was coming to the realization that I really wanted that. I was way too young to live the rest of my life without having fulfilling sex and intimacy.

Fortunately, we were able to discuss our marital challenges openly and without drama. After going to counseling and enduring many long difficult conversations, we agreed to separate while we could maintain a friendship and keep things amicable. We had traveled halfway around the world to bring home two children from Russia and didn't want our divorce to make them feel abandoned or without a cohesive family. Although it was difficult at the time, I appreciate how easy he made it and how we continue to work together as a team. I will always consider my ex-husband to be family and one of my closest friends. He has my back, even when I don't deserve it, and I am grateful for him.

I was, however, completely naïve and unprepared for the challenges of single parenting and starting over from scratch in my forties. We had joint custody, so I did not receive child support. We agreed on a small amount of alimony so I could be more available for the kids and not work the sixty-hour weeks that I did before children. I gave him many of the household possessions and furniture so that my kids wouldn't go without, and I was the one that went into debt to replace everything. In hindsight, I probably gave up more than I needed to, but my priority was to keep things amicable. We sold our home in an upside-down real estate market, so we were lucky to break even. Because I wasn't yet working, my ex even had to cosign the lease on my new home. I could only afford a two-bedroom, so my kids shared a room for a few years and honestly seemed to enjoy it. The only assets I had to my name were a fully paid-off SUV, a small savings account, and an IRA. But I had an MBA and great job skills, so I knew I could make a living. I just didn't know how to do it as a single parent. I had no family to help with the kids (other than my ex) and couldn't afford baby sitters or after-school programs. I had to find something that allowed me the flexibility to work around my kids' schedule yet would still cover the high cost of living in Southern California.

I was recruited quickly once I was in the job market and ultimately agreed to open an insurance agency. Most of my professional career was in the insurance and financial services industry, so it seemed like something I could at least consider without too much risk. Both of my parents owned their own businesses, and I had seen the good, the bad, and the ugly of their business challenges while growing up. As a result, I had always embraced the relative security of a corporate job and steady paycheck. It was never part of my life plan to start a business from scratch midlife as a single parent, but here I was, doing just that. My ex supported the idea, knowing that I would initially struggle more financially, but that it was better for the kids. He even agreed to be my first customer. I was hesitant starting off, not sure if I had made the right choice and had a hard time transitioning to being self-employed. I had to learn a whole new set of skills as far as structuring my day, being disciplined, being resilient (especially after bad days), learning how to market myself, and learning how to become a salesperson who wasn't too "salesy." I was also competing in a historically male-dominated field. The most successful agents I knew were men whose wives worked for them and ran the office, so they could focus entirely on sales. Finding female, single-parent mentors was difficult. I was also unprepared for how long it would take to start showing a profit and building residual income. I considered bankruptcy twice and probably should have just proceeded with it. However, my pride got in the way both times, and I was determined to dig myself out on my own. In hindsight, I know I made an emotional choice rather than a practical one. It made my life a lot more difficult as a result, but I'm at peace with my choice.

Around the time that I was starting the business, I met someone through an online dating site. I had tried the online thing for a few weeks and found it overwhelming, weird, and quite comical. Just as I was getting ready to call it quits, this one guy reached out to me who seemed genuine and different from the others. We went out and clicked right away, the best first date I'd ever had. He was also recently divorced and had two children a little older than mine. We had similar outlooks, values, and parenting styles, and an intense physical attraction. After living for so long without a healthy physical relationship, I was excited to find someone who I thought was the whole package. We agreed to take it slow and not bring the kids into it until we felt things were serious. He did still have a lot of anger toward his ex, and I had some initial concerns about his readiness for a relationship. He told me what I wanted to hear, and I blissfully ignored my gut and plunged head and heart first into the relationship.

After three months of dating, I met his kids. A few weeks after that, all four kids met, and from day one it was the most amazing blend of personalities I'd ever seen. You hear horror stories about trying to bring two families together, yet when the six of us were together, it just worked. We respected the other parent in the equation and the boundaries that go along with that. The four kids genuinely liked each other and enjoyed spending time together. Shortly after that, we started meeting parents, ex-spouses and extended families and within four or five months, this was very much a relationship with serious potential. We lived an hour away from each other and had opposite work schedules, but we were committed to making the effort and making it work. The relationship was a very healing blessing for two families who were still dealing with the aftermath of divorce.

I was forty-four at this point and started having a few unexpected physical challenges. I was active and athletic my entire life with dance, cheer, skiing, and as a part-time fitness instructor. I always had a low-grade nagging pain in my right hip and treated it as an overuse injury. I saw sports doctors and several specialists who kept me active and moving through the pain. Eventually one doctor started asking different questions and ordered an MRI. Turned out that the long-time overuse injury was actually a birth defect that required a full hip replacement. As shocked as I was to find out I needed major surgery so early in life, I was anxious to tackle the issue and put the pain behind me. I was at the point where my kids had to help me put my shoes on, and simple tasks such as bending over to do laundry or load the dishwasher were becoming unbearable.

I found an amazing surgeon who specialized in athletes. Although he had a waiting list, the few extra months of pain were worth the wait. I was walking hours after surgery and was in spin class five weeks after surgery. Because of my prior level of fitness, my recovery was quick, and the pain was gone. My biggest challenge was finding my new "normal" in terms of what I could and couldn't do. I didn't want to hold myself back because of fear, but I also had to honor my recovery process. It took a full year to get there, but I've been able to maintain an active lifestyle with only a few modifications. I am now five years post-surgery and have started climbing mountains (ten-thousand-footers) without any pain or restrictions. My other hip will also need to be replaced at some point in the next few years, but I will approach that surgery with the same positive attitude and will not hesitate to get it done.

About fifteen months after my hip surgery, my doctor recommended a hysterectomy due to my ongoing cancer scares. I was feeling quite strong after my hip recovery and really had no reservations about the hysterectomy. I had a long, trusting relationship with my doctor and didn't feel the need for a second opinion. It made sense; I'd been dealing with this situation since my teens. I was done with my uterus (it had never worked right anyway), and there was simply no reason to keep it. The plan was to leave my ovaries intact to delay menopause, especially since I was still young and had some bone and joint issues. Unfortunately, I really came to regret my decision. The surgery was invasive and much more traumatic, both physically and emotionally, than I ever expected. Because I never carried a baby to full term, my internal organs needed to be moved quite aggressively to get my uterus out. That resulted in abdominal and bowel pain that lasted almost nine months. I think there is also an unrealistic expectation when ovaries are left behind. I assumed I would have no hormonal or emotional impact whatsoever. Nothing could have been further from the truth. I was in pain and on an emotional rollercoaster for months. Given my prior pregnancy struggles, I had always considered myself a reproductive failure. My uterus was the enemy, and I thought I would be glad to get rid of it, so I was floored by the unexpected aftermath. Luckily there was no cancer, and my future risk of cancer had been diminished significantly with the surgery. However, as I write this, it has been four and a half years since the hysterectomy. I just had my first abnormal pap smear, and it has sent me into a tailspin of old emotions. As much as I hated the surgery and recovery, I realize that for the first time in my life, I'd had four and a half years of normal pap smears with no cancer scares, and it was awesome. Now I am right back into the world of biopsies and waiting, and I'm running out of removable parts. As always, I will do my best to stay positive and deal with whatever comes my way, but some days are easier than others. The good news is I am now fifty and have not yet started menopause, so at least that part of the plan seems to have worked.

Throughout both surgeries, my boyfriend was by my side, but like me, he had a harder time with the second recovery. His father also passed away between my two surgeries, so he was emotionally drained from caring for him. We were hitting the two-and-a-half-year mark on our relationship, and I think that other strains were starting to show. We were fighting more, and not productively. We were both drinking more than we should and were making less effort to see each other. Instead of dealing with it like the mature adult that I knew I was, I let myself get insecure. As my self-esteem suffered, I relied on the relationship to provide validation in my life. I became needy, started gaining weight, and pretty much set aside my own wants and needs to do whatever he wanted. We did go to counseling, and it helped for a while, but we were really starting to struggle with even basic communication. He stonewalled any attempt to talk about our future and shut down even more, which, of course, only made me more insecure and needy. I was turning into a person I didn't like because of the relationship but couldn't get out of my own way. It seemed like the only time we would relax and give each other a break is if we had a drink or six. The physical aspect was still strong and probably the only thing holding us together, but the relationship was on shaky ground and so was I.

We agreed to take a short break which only lasted about six weeks with daily communication. We did get back together, and things were good for a while, but then he started to draw back again. He stopped coming to work events, started coming to my house less, and started pulling away physically (unless he was drinking). Rather than do the right thing and end things, I tried to do all the relationship work for both of us. I made excuses for his behavior and figured if I just changed myself enough, he would engage again. Instead I became depressed and suicidal and started doing crazy things just to get his attention. I didn't know how to stop myself and regain my dignity. Then I think God sent me a gift in a very unexpected manner. I found out that he had slept with someone else during our "break." This boyfriend, who had been cheated on by his ex and who would preach about loyalty to anyone who would listen, had slept with someone else! And shockingly, I wasn't mad. It was exactly the wake-up call I needed to take my power back. It made me realize that I had given all my power to a man who didn't value or deserve it. I did try to talk to him about it, which of course went badly, but it was just a matter of time after that. Even so, I went to counseling to make sure I wasn't making a "rash" decision and gave him more chances than he deserved (as I have done with almost every important relationship in my life). After six years together, I ended it calmly and unemotionally, and I have never felt stronger, more relieved, heathier, or more proud of myself.

Another big catalyst for me was the prospect of turning fifty. From the moment I turned forty-nine, everything started to change. I began to panic and had the feeling I was running out of time. I had to find my life's purpose, find my life partner, get back in shape, stop everything from sagging, address all my demons, and achieve financial success—all before I turned fifty. It was as if I'd strapped myself with this extreme deadline and ungodly pressure. I had to figure out everything about my life in one year or less. I knew I didn't want to wake up at fifty-five and find myself in the same relationship wondering if it had a future, so for that the deadline was good. I started to realize that all the daily crap I was stressing over wasn't getting me anywhere productive and was only burning me out. I also realized that there were some selfish, toxic people in my life who only showed up when they needed something. As a fiftieth birthday present to myself, I started to eliminate those people from my life first. I also gave myself permission to draw healthier boundaries with family, friends, clients, and anyone else who potentially needed or wanted something from me. I was sacrificing too much of myself to please these people with little to no return, and I recognized I am no good to anyone if I am tired, emotionally drained, and bitter. I also gave myself permission to be a little selfish and start putting myself first because if I'm happy, everyone benefits! And I started talking to myself differently. I was very guilty of years of negative self-talk and realized I was much nicer to other people than I was to myself. That internal dialog had to change, and I started talking to myself the way I would talk to other people. I do still struggle a bit with self-limiting beliefs and thinking I'm not worthy of success or amazing relationships, but I'm working on it.

I was a total train wreck right up until my fiftieth birthday, literally right up until the latter part of that day. I decided to take my kids away for a few days rather than sit home and be sad. I was cranky and irritable and got worse as the day approached. On the actual day, once I knew I made it through most of the day, I started to relax. Then the next day, I realized I was still the same person and nothing had really changed except I had given myself all these awesome thought-changing gifts. The anxiety of turning fifty was so much worse than the reality of it. I felt this huge burden lift off my chest and found this amazing feeling of enlightenment and peace. I felt happy and healthier than ever; I even felt physically lighter. Even though I'm still not in the shape I'd like to be, I feel sexier and more confident than I have in years, and that confidence is sexy enough to overcome a few extra pounds any day. At fifty, it is so liberating to finally accept myself and make the most of what I have and who I am. And despite all the pain, for the first time in my life, I feel capable of true, open, honest love because I know myself better and know what I want. I think in my forties I still dated like I did before marriage and kids, applying the same old beliefs because I didn't know any better. At fifty, I realize that I am a grown-ass woman who has her shit (almost) together, and that is sexier than anything I could have offered in my forties. I honestly love being fifty and truly believe I am just starting to blossom. The birthday I feared the most ended up giving me the best gift ever—myself. Do I occasionally struggle with loneliness? Absolutely. I am usually the only single person at every work, family, or social event. Sometimes I love it, and other times, I really let it bother me. The best I can do is just take it day by day and wake up every morning with a fresh attitude.

What I wish I had known . . . and what my advice is to you, the reader

- First and foremost, trust your gut. Your gut is your best friend and it never lies. It always knows the truth.

- Pleasing others at your own expense is unhealthy and never works. You end up tired and bitter, and they will not appreciate you for it or change their behavior.

- You are so much more attractive when you are peaceful, confident, and happy. It is the best gift you can give yourself and others. It is worth every effort in your life to find that feeling and never let it go.

- Some stress can be healthy and help you achieve great things, but know your limits.

- Nothing you do will change another person or their behavior. You can only control yourself, your own behavior, and how you choose to react to people or situations. Stay classy, take the high road, and always be gracious—you will never regret it.

- Let other people own their shit. Do not take responsibility for their problems or behavior. No matter how much they try to manipulate you, the only one responsible for them is them.

- Never give another person control of your life or your future. Nobody cares about your life more than you do, so own it and create your own path. You will need to make adjustments along the way, but it's your life and your life only.

- Always believe in yourself; you are stronger than you think, and you will get through whatever life throws at you. Some days you might just need to pull the covers over your head and try again tomorrow, but don't worry, you got this.

- Learn from your past but let it go. Don't let it define or control you. Get counseling, do whatever it takes to process it, and move on.

- A little isolation is okay, but too much is not good. I am an introvert by nature and tend to withdraw when troubled. I am learning to surround myself with good people and lean on them when needed. You may not always take their advice, but the good people in your life will always help you sort out your thoughts.

- Journal or find a way to capture your thoughts. I finally embraced this after starting my own business. I forced myself to write down each day's victories no matter how small, in order to stay positive and optimistic. As I started having internal conversations with myself about relationships or big decisions, I would write them down, even if it just meant typing notes on my phone. A journal is always there to listen. It's incredible how journaling your thoughts helps you make sense of them. And once those thoughts are out, they no longer physically drain you either. I reviewed my journals and notes while writing this and was thrilled that I could read through the ones written on my darkest days and read them without pain. It shows me how far I've come.

- Finally, you are beautiful in your own unique way, so just be the best possible you. We don't all look like supermodels and may not fit the conventional definition of beauty, but there is something unique, special, and appealing about every person. I bet you could people-watch for hours and find something nice to say about everyone who walked by. Now do the same for yourself. Someone out there thinks you are the most amazing person in the world. See yourself through their eyes even if only for a few minutes. Don't try to change or be someone else.

BE KIND TO YOURSELF

Introduction

I ask you, the reader, to pay attention to a key word that recurs over and over again in my story and consider it when you are done reading. For you see, I recently learned something from a person who is younger than me. I learned that your attitude toward the things in life, good or bad, is so important. It's not that I haven't heard this before, or read it many times, and even tried to practice it. It is that my perception of what I have experienced since I turned forty has altered since I learned this important lesson. I will explain more at the end.

Since I turned forty, I have done so many things I *never* even contemplated as a possibility before . . . I got two tattoos, ran three half marathons (OK, I "ran" two and limped through the last one, which has its own importance in my story), ran various 10Ks, and read a lot: multiple self-help books, books on perimenopause and menopause, articles about all things menopause, articles on healing, articles on nutrition and healthy organic food options, and articles on "why you are overweight regardless of having run a half marathon." My focus since I turned forty has been almost obsessively surviving, trying to overcome being forty and older . . . and not repeating past mistakes.

At the age of forty-seven, and as I was writing this, I really wish I could tell the woman I was then (in my thirties transitioning to my forties) what I know now. I wonder if she would listen, or at least take some of the advice to help her avoid some of the pain, anger, self-deprecating thoughts, ego-driven decisions, and, at times, the loss of laughter. All mostly done for the sake of surviving. More importantly, I would like to help her find the road to herself again, which includes dropping judgment from her vocabulary (this is a very difficult task, I might say, as society often encourages it in various ways). To be kind and accepting of herself so she can be accepting of others. You see, these last seven years have been a rollercoaster. Obviously, God wanted me to learn something. To appreciate something. I thought it was me, but it is life. It is all things in life, including those we love whether close or far. It is that kindness and love can help us to forgive and accept, and, to stop judging ourselves and others . . . because they are not like us.

Me before Forty

I look back on my life and know that up to the age of twenty-two, I had focus: college, career, and a well laid out plan. My childhood, for all that was good, there was much that was not; I was riddled with instability and fear, including circumstances I just had to survive. Literally survive. I admit I denied it for years, even running from it, but I did learn to accept my early childhood and move on from it. Part of running from it was having the idea that my way out was through an education. Hence the well laid out plan. However, in my early twenties, I got married, had to turn down two jobs, moved to California, got divorced, started to reconnect with myself (divorce takes its toll on you), and at the end of my twenties, ran my own business. I met my current husband when I was twenty-nine, but wouldn't date him until I was thirty-one. Taking on five step-children and an ex-wife is daunting. He was in the middle of his divorce when we first met, a bit older than me, and with kids (which was on my "no" list . . . you know, those lists we make). In the end, though, I allowed the door to open for us to be more than friends not long after I turned thirty-one. I went with my instincts instead of the list. I took on the role of stepmom of five kids and transitioned to a career that I still do well in today. The key to this is, in doing all of this, I put aside my dreams. No one asked me to, but I did it because I felt it was the right thing to do at the time.

I was happy during this period of my life. I was happier than I had ever been in my life, even with certain struggles mixed in. My husband and I were the best of friends, in it together; and his kids liked me (I had no intention of trying to replace their mom, which made things easier). We loved a good bottle of wine (often) and having friends over. At the end of my thirties though, my view on life started to shift as our world started to change. It wasn't any one thing, really, although I can say, and my husband would probably agree, the catalyst was my husband losing his job . . . then it was the loss of his next job, at the height of the Great Recession. Our life started to shift beneath our feet. His lifelong career was in a dying industry. The Great Recession only made it worse. During my late thirties, I became the primary supporter of the family, and my husband began to drink heavily because he couldn't find a job.

Further, around this time, my mother, who I was not close to at this point of my life, died from cancer. I mourned the loss, but she really had not been a mother to me growing up, and I accepted that. Some of you may think "how is that possible?" My answer, my stepmom. She has been more of a mother than my mother. It isn't that I didn't care about my mother; it's just that when someone hurts you more than loves you, and you don't understand the "why" behind it until many years later. You end up putting aside society's ideas of how it should be. I only hope she has peace now. The cards had been stacked against my real mom as a child born during World War II in the Netherlands. That is another story, though.

Last, but not least, during the turmoil of these later years of my thirties, we had to put our beautiful dog to sleep. She was fourteen years old, and I think with the loss of her, on top of everything else, I lost hope in life for a period of time.

So I barreled into my forties battling depression. The financial strains, my husband's depression, including his alcoholism, and the losses made me angry and resentful. It was a form of death of my former self. In this weakened state, I had the tendency to make most decisions based on fear, ego, and trying to find some happiness for me and my husband again. Physically my health was faltering as well. Brain fog had set in, some memory loss (words when I needed them most), occasional hot flashes, increased occurrence of migraines, change in pattern of my monthly cramps (often they would last up to three or four days, hitting me at random times and impacting my job), and flares of fibromyalgia lasting longer than ever before.

My Journey Post-Forty (Intertwined Emotional and Physical)

I am a firm believer that God puts people in our lives for a reason and also sends challenges to help us learn to live in hope. On the other hand, when we don't put our faith in him, we try to control and make circumstances worse than they need to be. We try to make it what *we* want it to be . . . based on ego and fear. The choice to follow ego has been a fault of mine. The same with fear. I admit it. I always put them under the umbrella of "do it to survive." During this phase of my life, I tried to control everything, including thinking I could help my husband and his depression while trying to tackle my own. They were connected in my mind. In the process, for several years, I lost myself and my faith . . . but I always fought to recover it and to live. I searched everywhere for that elusive missing happiness.

Within a year after I turned forty, the recession continued its ugly hold on America and us—we sold the house as a short sale, were financially devastated, and moved to Northern California . . . for a job . . . for me . . . for a fresh start. Only two of the kids were under eighteen now, and we believed that it was a good move. I was offered significantly more money, and my husband would be closer to his brother. The thing with a fresh start is, if you are embarrassed about your past and/or battling depression, it isn't fresh for long. We stayed stuck in our past. In addition, I struggled to get my husband help while also unintentionally enabling him. I worked for one of the best companies in the Bay Area but often failed to fully appreciate it.

Regardless of the good parts of my life, I struggled to breathe. I often woke up in the middle of the night with anxiety attacks thinking about all those things I never really could change or influence, but replaying them over and over again, including how I could fix the various aspects of our life that weren't "perfect." I desperately wanted my husband to be happy, and I believed if he was, then he would stop drinking so much.

The first year in Northern California, I got pneumonia and was often sick with other ailments. So, what does someone do to pull themselves out? Usually, they seek counseling. Well, after reading an article about training for half marathons, I thought, *Maybe I could try a 10K*. I told myself, *If I train slow, build up slow, why not?* It was also a way to heal after having pneumonia. That was the start of my obsession with running. Before long it was something I owned as mine. The first thing in years that was for me and me alone. I didn't want or have to share it with anyone. I was doing it for myself. It hurt at times, but oh, it felt so good, even with the fibromyalgia, which made my training take twice as long as most people require. I also had to manage those times out running when I started my period—which meant cramps. I trained slow and steady. It didn't cure all my ailments, but it took me on a road to find hope again. I had to prove to myself that those physical ailments really did not control me.

I found that as I trained, I also grew distant from my husband. I was slowly not doing everything for him and the kids. I wasn't obsessing over him. I was looking at myself and thinking, *It's okay if you need to buy a new pair of running shoes . . . It's okay if you don't buy that for one of the girls . . . It's okay if you don't want to talk to your husband because he is drunk again.* I loved them, but I knew I needed to find a way to get back to myself. I was doing well at work, but I probably should have been an actor since, if anyone really noticed, I was a fake, a lost individual—like I was treading water most of the time. The moments of breathing were good and lifesaving—a vacation, a good run, a visit with friends. The good parts kept me from drowning in woe-is-me thoughts.

These first few years in Northern California were my transition period to reconnect with myself. I think now that I was like a toddler learning to walk. Only someone who has been devastated financially can relate to what I am saying here. It was also a period where my best friend, my husband, was faltering in his life. No matter what I did to try to control our circumstances, it drove him away or just enabled his behavior. Finally, I discovered Al Anon after his first attempt to get sober. It was a step in the right direction for me. It helped me realize his demons were his and not mine. I learned to detach and disconnect most of the time. Sometimes, I would fall into old habits, but would pull myself back to the core principle of detachment.

Regardless of the struggles, during those four and a half years of living just outside San Francisco, I found some personal strength I never imagined I had. As I mentioned earlier, these were things I had never contemplated I could do before. I ran my first half marathon on the hills of San Francisco and raised money for the Leukemia & Lymphoma Society (LLS), while training with Team in Training. I did it again the next year. It took mental strength as much as physical. I, for myself, and no one else, proved that I could endure, that my migraines, endometriosis and fibromyalgia did not control me. Further, that while living a life where I hid most of my personal struggles and stress from the people I worked with, my friends and my own family, I could still do something positive. I regained a sense of myself for short periods at a time, but, unfortunately, found I could not hold it for long. Detachment from my husband's struggles was one thing; being comfortable with myself again was another.

Stress—it controls you if you don't control it. It can affect every cell in your body, they say. It can ravage a woman going through perimenopause. As most women know, when we step into our forties, a good many of us are entering perimenopause. The changes are subtle to some and not so subtle to others. For me personally, in having discussions with other women, including my amazing gynecologist in the Bay Area, I learned that I had actually started to have perimenopausal symptoms in my late thirties. Was it the stress that made it start early? Was it the fact that I had never been pregnant? I can't say. I just know my memory issues and hot flashes started around age thirty-eight. I started to use a natural balance progesterone cream (close to, but not exactly like, bioidentical creams, which are ideal) around age forty-one, which helped me significantly. It was a highly recommended brand, and my doctor approved of it. It helped my monthly cramps caused by endometriosis (I wish I had known about it in my twenties). I refused to use any prescribed progestin pill (which is not bioidentical and, from what I researched, has side effects I did not want). The balance cream also helped the night sweats which started around age forty-two. I still use the cream today. It hasn't cured the things my body was experiencing and continues to go through, but the symptoms are less taxing on me. I am also less anxious when I use it. All that stress for all those years, well that took its toll. My husband may have been battling his own demons, but he would say that I wasn't exactly pleasant when I wasn't using the cream. My anxiety and high-stress response to things drove people away. I physically manifested my emotions. I truly believe that. I was angry more often than not. It was as if a dark cloud hovered over me. However, the brain fog I'd experienced for years, and which got progressively worse with the stress, was the most difficult. The progesterone cream helped with some of the brain fog, but I can't say it has helped my memory.

Further, on the physical front, you may be thinking, "Wow, I bet you were really fit and slim during this phase of your life with all that running." I would say, "Kind of." The running helped me, it is true, but I was still, every year, gaining more weight around my midsection. My joints hurt more than ever, and I felt tired most of the time. Part of it was the fibromyalgia which usually "flares" up in phases for me, triggered by extreme weather fluctuations or high stress. The progesterone helped, but so did taking vitamin D3. Trying a raw diet was fine, as was juicing. Nothing, however, stopped the weight gain.

I honestly believe that much of my pain, weight gain, and anger could have been better addressed if I had just been able to find a way to control my stress. While I was "surviving" and trying not to drown, I would blame my work, I would blame a reaction of a friend to my behavior, I would blame my husband, I would blame the kids, I would blame, I would blame, I would blame. I was playing the victim.

What good was all that blame? Nothing came out of it. It was my ego trying to control all these outside factors, which in turn hurt me physically and mentally. One of the best things I did on this path to discovery was read Eckhart Tolle's book, *The Power of Now*. Although I wasn't quite ready for his message when I first read it, I did find myself realizing how my ego dictated so much of what I did, including my reaction to my circumstances. I slowly started to bring myself back to a focus on what was happening around me both physically and mentally at that moment, rather than getting lost in "woe is me, look at what we went through," or what I sacrificed for the people I loved, or even thinking some future moment would solve everything. It was a step in the right direction, but if you don't practice it every day, then you can easily fall back into old patterns . . . especially for someone who had been struggling with what life had brought, some of it as a result of decisions I'd made years before. I did supplement my running with yoga to gain some peace, however, running was my sanctuary.

This leads me to my next challenge—my last half marathon. When I trained for this half marathon, I did it on my own. I had learned a lot from the Team in Training coaching and felt confident that I could manage without any support or team. I felt physically strong on my last twelve-mile training run. I thought, *I am ready for this half marathon—more so than any of the others*. In the end, however, that last half marathon was the toughest of the three I finished, and why I am going into details about this run over the others. During the run, I knew by mile four that my body was not agreeing with what I wanted to accomplish. For the first time in all my runs, from training to actual events, I thought multiple times, *Should I call my husband to pick me up?* This was as nausea settled in, then my right hip flexor completely went south (because my posture and gait deteriorated) and, finally, I started limping down hills. Something in me always said, *No, just keep going.* I finished, but I would have preferred crawling across the finish line. Instead, I attempted a slow limp/jog. I still have pain in that hip from that event, but I don't regret that I forced myself to finish. I just haven't been able to run for more than four mile run since.

The details of this last half marathon are more important than the first two for one reason—because of what happened to me mentally afterward. I struggled to regain that "thing" running and training had given me. That one thing that was my sanctuary, my form of meditation, was no longer available to me. My body wouldn't allow it, so my brain soon followed where my body took me. The time worn path of "woe is me" returned in full force.

The ego can take over in so many ways if you let it. As can fear. Since I couldn't run, I needed to fix things . . . you know, since we all can control what others do and think. Can't we?

In the meantime, what had been somewhat affordable for the Bay Area location was now becoming, at a fast pace, less affordable. My husband had started to have some success as an abstract artist up there, but our combined earnings were not enough for us to live comfortably. We never fully got to a point of feeling financially safe. After our experience four years earlier, it was tiring for both of us to feel constantly strapped, so we started to consider other places to live. We chose to move back and be near the kids in Southern California. I also needed help with my husband's increased use of alcohol.

During this move, I dealt with many of my own demons and have experienced much self-reflection. My husband, through a difficult process for him, found sobriety with the help of his siblings. What has helped me daily to manage my stress, as we fought for the insurance to cover his inpatient stay, is meditation. I can't run the distances I once did, but I now combine yoga, short runs, and early morning guided meditation to help me manage my stress. Meditation really has been life changing for me. Learning to do it daily was a struggle at first, but then I started to catch those moments of connection and peace they talk about . . . and I wanted more. I do it every morning and I can say my husband is also grateful for it!

When you start down the path of self-awareness, it is amazing the things you intentionally hide from yourself and are willing to try. All those years, the one thing I failed to admit to was that my "go to" in times of stress was always sugar, and mostly in the form of candy or cookies. I craved it. I would even hide it so people wouldn't know what an addict I was. I believed it helped in moments of stress, but it really just made me sick. I juiced, I am gluten free, I tried the raw diet, almost all my food is organic, we only use non-toxic cleaners in the house, and more . . . but, outside of wheat, the most devastating thing to me physically has been sugar, something I'd never eliminated before. It controlled me. It was my addiction. It wasn't until a nutritionist helped guide me through the steps in eliminating sugar from my diet that I felt less pain, less anxiety, and fewer highs and lows. I can honestly say removing it has helped my monthly cycle (although it still is not consistent, starting early, lasting as long as a week one month and only a few days the next). The only thing elimination of sugar didn't help was my hip flexor!

I am 98 percent sugar free today, and I've lost most of the weight I put on over the last seven years . . . and I eat more than I did before (my husband can attest to this). The difference is, I now eat mostly organic, nutritional whole food. I am categorized as prediabetic; my glucose levels reflect it, so I need to be my own advocate. My family is prone to it. It's in the genes. My paternal grandmother went blind from complications associated with it and then died from related issues. My aunt had it and died from complications associated with it. My father and my oldest brother and sister struggle with it, and on and on. I don't want diabetes. If eliminating sugar accomplishes it, then I don't regret the loss of those cookies, that candy bar, or a handful of chocolate covered Gummy Bears. There are natural good substitutes, and occasionally I will have a bite of gluten-free cake or a piece of dark chocolate. It is enough. As I approach my fifties, I feel better than I have in years—both physically and mentally. I am making my health a priority now. I have also learned how to say no.

As to my next phase of my journey, I look now to helping my father and stepmom. This, I know, is necessary. My father is at a phase in his life where signs of dementia appear in most conversations with him, and my stepmom needs help to take care of him. It is something I don't shy away from, but do have a heavy heart about, as would most people under similar circumstances.

What I wish I had known . . . and what my advice is to you, the reader

As I stated earlier, you see the recurring theme of "surviving" through my story and driving so many things in my life up to my mid-forties. However, as I write this, my niece, at age twenty-nine, has conveyed to me a wisdom that can only come from someone who is facing death. She has a certainty of knowing how much time she has left, as she has stage 3 pancreatic cancer. She accepts it; but is still fighting it. She isn't just surviving; she is embracing the little things. She is, as my father said, an angel who asks for nothing. She applauds the nurses and doctors who have been helping her and, as her sister said, have only been kind and courageous.

My own experiences have been about surviving my life. "I survived" is what I said, as though that was strength. What is "I survived"? I said it as though I had fought death and defeated it in those years from my twenties to my forties. True, I had struggles, but if you really look at them, most were self-inflicted.

You see, through a simple conversation, a shift happened in me. I realized that my niece is a fighter, but she also accepts she will die. She is not playing a victim to her illness, her situation, or the fact that only now has family become part of her life again. She possesses a peace that comes from a different realm than what the rest of us tend to live in. I can honestly say I don't even know all she has endured in her life, but in talking to her, she lives in her truth. For those of us who meditate, she has, simply by being her, that which I believe we all try to attain.

From a personal perspective, with all the changes that happen to us during this period of our life, from a change of focus of raising kids, to aging parents, to career ups and downs (ours and others), I would say, be kind to yourself. Food is not the only answer or problem. It is a pleasure item, but really, it is for sustenance. Also know that alcohol will never solve your problems. It is a destructive mechanism to numb yourself. Limit its use. Realize that someone else's inability to accept themselves and their life is their ego resisting their life . . . and it isn't yours to control or fix. Forgive yourself and others, but more importantly, live in the now. Look around you at this moment in time and realize the beauty, even if it isn't how you wanted or envisioned it. Meditate daily (whatever form you choose). Stop that ego voice in your head that takes you backwards reliving pain and happiness in the past or makes you think that you can control the future. Accept what is, do what you love, and leave it in God's hands. He is always with you. This doesn't mean you have to be passive, by no means. Is my niece being passive by accepting, but still fighting? No. Am I being passive by writing and telling you this story, my story? No.

You see, when I say I am writing, that is not a small statement . . . I am saying that I have reconnected with *my* dreams. I am reconnecting with myself and my truth.

Whatever happens next, I also know I have choices. For some reason, I never really thought I did before, but now I embrace this notion.

EXPLORING THE WORLD

From war and immigration to a startup founder. This is my story.

Me before Forty

I am an immigrant and, as such, I had to deal with all the struggles that come with leaving your beloved but war-torn home country, including learning to love a new culture, language, and way of life. It is pretty lonely when no one looks like you or speaks your language. I was eighteen when I moved to the United States. I traveled halfway around the world alone, with nothing but hopes of security, education, and job opportunities.

I worked really hard, including earning my undergraduate degree and taking any other opportunity I could find to learn more. I studied computer science and entered corporate America working my way up the ladder, got my MBA, and worked some more. I discovered my love of travel and adventure along the way. My twenties were about the single life, including the freedom of traveling the world and having different outdoor adventures every weekend. I got my heart broken multiple times along the way, but finally met my prince charming in graduate school. I got married, and my thirties were focused on settling down and playing house. During this period of my life, my husband and I both had high paying jobs in Silicon Valley that included stock options and an investment portfolio which made us virtual millionaires. We were flying high. Until.

When the stock market crashed in the late 1990s and early 2000, we pretty much lost everything. We both got laid off, our portfolio all but disappeared, and the value of our house crashed. It was a hard time in the tech world. That's when we decided to pack up and leave Silicon Valley. We moved to sunny San Diego. We had no job prospects and just figured we would build a new life there. The job opportunities were not spectacular in San Diego and, without a network, it took us a long time to get settled, but we loved the beach lifestyle and enjoyed our time together.

My Emotional and Physical Journey Post-Forty

We had our two daughters when I was in my late thirties, and I turned forty with a new baby at my breast and a three-year-old toddler. I took a four-month leave from my project management job to care for my second child when she was a newborn, but when she turned four months old, I looked at the infant who was so attached to her mother, and I just couldn't leave her for eight to ten hours a day and go back to work. I was old enough to understand and appreciate the value of time with kids and that they grow up way too fast. I had already been feeling so guilty leaving my toddler at daycare every day. Oh, how as a career woman I struggled with being a mother! The mother instinct won in the end, and I quit my job in favor of caring for my children. For the next two years, I enjoyed every minute of being a mom to my girls, did lots of mommy-and-me playdates, and happily played the role of a San Diego housewife.

However, living in Scripps Ranch, the upscale suburb of San Diego, the materialistic pressures were all too present. My husband's single, low income put our family of four below the poverty line according to the California definitions of wealth. We didn't have health insurance, and I had to take my kids to the free clinics for their checkups and shots. Luckily, the sale of our Bay Area home gave enough savings to sustain us for a while. A good friend once told me, "When you have time, you have no money, and when you have money, you have no time." It's really up to us to choose one over the other. For me, the choice was clear at the time, but it was many years later that I finally understood the man-made concept of money and when to accept "enough." The book *The Soul of Money: Transforming Your Relationship with Money and Life* by Lynne Twist was instrumental in this transformation of life for me.

My body changed as I entered my forties. I was always exhausted and figured it was taking care of two little kids that was making me so tired. Some afternoons I couldn't keep my eyes open. My kids would be playing in the living room, and I would nod off on the couch. When I finally dragged myself to the doctor, she told me I had thyroid issues. In addition, I had the early signs of cervical cancer that needed to be dealt with. They took out as much as they could from my cervix, but it spread and was threatening my uterus and my life. They informed me that I needed a hysterectomy and would not be able to have any more children. It was a scary time in my life as a woman. It felt like I'd be losing my femininity. Emotionally, I was a mess. My hormones were fluctuating, and I was worried about my children's well-being if I couldn't take care of them anymore. The only consolation was that we already had two kids and were not planning to have any more.

This is when my husband was suddenly laid off, and the little income we had all but disappeared. It was hard not to get drawn into the depths of despair. It felt like a black hole had opened, and I was falling deeper and deeper into it. Some days it was hard to get out of bed. Why me? Why again? The questions kept circulating in my head. First revolution and war followed by the struggles of immigration. Then losing all we had worked so hard for and having to start over in San Diego from scratch . . . and now this. If it wasn't for the needs of my girls, I might have never pulled myself out of that hole.

I had to do something! I couldn't just sit idle. I had to pull myself together and find a job. I'd been out of the market for over two years, and my experience was obsolete. Companies wanted to know what I had been doing for the last two years. How do you answer that? I'd been a mommy? I knew I had to get creative and reinvent myself.

I organized my thoughts and pushed myself out of the house and back to the professional world. I started networking and volunteering. I joined the Project Management Institute (PMI) and began studying for the coveted PMP certification. My peers had corporate training funds paying for their $2,000 prep class that I couldn't afford. I organized myself into a daily four-hour studying routine for three months and took as many mock exams as I could. The failure rate was over 50 percent for the four-hour certification exam, but I ended up passing the first time I took it. I found my drive and got my energy back. The PMI community encouraged me, and I found a job as a project manager at a startup with the help of a friend. A year later, I landed a great job at Intuit, one of the biggest employers in San Diego, and was back on my feet again. I had pulled my family out of bankruptcy, and that was a great feeling. I couldn't stop smiling.

My health issues were still there though. I had a hysterectomy at age for-ty-three, which put me straight from breastfeeding into early menopause! Those darn hormones are so important to your body. I started losing my hair. My beautiful long curly hair came out in handfuls. I had hot flashes and night sweats, and sex became unbearably painful. What is there to be done about menopause? Luckily, we have so many resources available to us. Research brought me to the natural treatment called bioidentical hor-mone therapy. The effects were almost instantaneous. All the symptoms went away, and I ended up using it for five years until all menopause symp-toms had passed. I highly recommend it to all women.

It didn't take long for stress of the job, two little kids, and home life to weigh down on me. As great as the pay was, the job was very demanding. The threat of getting fired was forever looming over us, as every three months scores of employees were being laid off. I also worried about my kids con-stantly and felt guilty leaving them in the care of nannies and babysitters. I fussed over finding the perfect nanny and interviewed an unlimited number of candidates. I would wake up at three in the morning, and my brain would circulate all kinds of thoughts in my head. I couldn't go back to sleep. Anxiety was gaining a hold on me.

My tendinitis issues that had put me into disability for a year in my twenties came back. I constantly had wrist pain from computer work, which affected both my job and my home life. I couldn't cut and stir for cooking. I couldn't lift my girls and hold them. My arms hurt! I got to a point where I was exhausted and constantly in pain.

In addition, I started having foot and leg issues to the point where I couldn't walk around the block. To understand how hard this was for me, you have to know my love of nature and adventure. Ten years earlier, I had hiked the Grand Canyon's eighteen-mile journey to the bottom and back up in one day. I love to hike, bike, ski, and explore every mountain. But at this point in my life, I couldn't even walk around the block. What could possibly be going on?

I started researching and looking for help—seeing doctor after doctor looking for answers. I was finally able to get to the root cause of the issues I was having: stress and anxiety! Too many hours of the day spent sitting and fighting issues at work. Stress built up in my neck, which in turn gave me headaches and blocked the flow of endorphins to my body. Not sleeping well, my body had no chance to heal itself at night either. My muscles were tightened into knots from stress and did not get a chance to relax. I was overwhelmed by life, and it was manifesting itself as physical symptoms.

I was lucky to find a doctor with the belief that your mind and body are related—that one affects the other. It's about a balanced lifestyle, release, and relief. I looked to yoga and meditation for relaxing both body and mind. I also found solace in nature walks. When I relaxed, took breaks, and walked, my pain was reduced. I learned the counterintuitive nature of healing. The more you move, the better you become. Our body is not built for sitting.

My doctor put me on a low dose of anxiety medication that not only relieved me from the pain, but helped me sleep at night and relax. She also referred me to a TMJ doctor who made me mouth appliances that brought my balance back and consequently healed my foot and leg issues. I was once again able to get out, hike, and enjoy nature.

My husband was also able to take on a good position, and we were back on our feet financially. We started taking nice vacations and introducing our girls to the beauty of nature around us. We went skiing in Utah; we spent summers boating on lakes and hiking the waterfalls of Yosemite. We went kayaking in Hawaii and snorkeling in Mexico. All along, we were watching our baby girls grow into beautiful little girls.

The "teen" issues with my older daughter started when she was ten. She had always been a sensitive child who needed a lot of attention, but now she was demanding my attention through negative behavior. I was forty-six years old, and my energy was declining. Coming home at six thirty every night and having to make dinner quickly for a starving family, I had no time to spend with my girls. Our routine was dinner, cleanup, bath, and bed. Through it all, I was exhausted from my day. I had no energy for my kids and would yell at them for every little thing. I was always asking "Why can't they just clean up after themselves without me asking?" and "How many times do I have to repeat something before they listen?" My younger child, however, would just hug me, which melted my heart. Meanwhile, my older one would fight back. She would answer back and throw a fit, yell and scream and cry. It made our home life miserable. It got to a point that I just wanted to pack my bag and run away from the house. I couldn't go on.

This was a new territory for me. Kids don't come with user manuals, and I had no training in psychology or how to deal with these kinds of issues. I had to get educated, and it had to be fast. My older daughter and I started getting help by going to therapy. I discovered that both the problem and the answer were me. I was the mom, the guardian, and the answer had to come from me. Kids react to their environment. By being exhausted all the time, I was not creating a nurturing environment. I was unhappy at work, and it was affecting our home life.

I hit a plateau at work and was not learning or challenged anymore. Every day was a repeat of the last, always fighting the same corporate battles. I didn't see a path up and started questioning what I was working for and whom I was helping. In a big corporation, many layers removed from the customer and lost in the politics of the company, it was hard for me to feel like I was fulfilling any purpose. I had always wanted to be an entrepreneur and loved technology innovations. I wanted to be closer to the innovation. I took on a side project working on a new idea at my company, with a young innovative team and had fun. I started thinking about ideas and how I could start something new, but I couldn't think of anything. Besides, I was way too busy with work and life to be able to add anything to an already full load.

Although we had become financially sound with both of us working, the financial anxiety was always looming around us if I even contemplated quitting my job. Can we afford for me not to bring in that second income? At age forty-eight, I started thinking about the big picture and asking questions: How many more years will I have the energy for this fast-paced corporate environment? When do I want to retire? Will we have enough money saved for retirement? We didn't really have a plan for our future— the girls' college, retirement, travel. Our money was sitting in multiple IRAs, ESPPs, RSUs, 401Ks with no order whatsoever. We were paying all kinds of hidden fees and didn't even know it.

Then a book motivated me to organize our finances. The book, *Money, Master the Game* by Tony Robbins, literally changed my life. He has a way of frustrating and putting a fire in you to make a change. It took a good nine months of interviewing financial analysts to finally find a suitable one for us, but within a year of my listening to that book, we'd consolidated all our accounts and had a solid plan. Looking at spreadsheets, we realized that we could indeed live comfortably on my husband's income and still give me time to start a business. The problem was, I still didn't have an idea for a business, so I kept on working at a job I didn't like, all stressed out and unhappy.

The answer came to me in a very roundabout way. It had to be a dramatic wakeup call, and life handed me one in a very painful way. We got the call at two in the morning—when bad news usually finds you. The one-hour drive from San Diego to Irvine was torturous. When we entered the hospital, we were hit with the news that my dad had passed away suddenly in the middle of the night after undergoing routine surgery. I didn't get to say good-bye.

It was like my whole world came crashing around me. When you look death in the face, everything else seems small and trivial. Time had run out for him, and it runs out for all of us. We tend to postpone our hopes and dreams thinking, *Someday* . . . . Well, that someday might never come if we keep postponing happiness. I learned a lot from my dad over the years, and he taught me this one last lesson with his passing, a lesson that has had a profound influence on how I live my life today.

I remember coming home when all the funeral activities were over and thinking, *My god I need to look at life differently. I need to spend more time doing what I love. I need to be available for life and not just get through it. I need to open my eyes and take in the joys of life that were all around me. I need to live my life* now.

My interests had always been travel and nature adventure. The idea came to me when we tried to plan a nature adventure trip to Wisconsin where my husband had gone to university. Not knowing anything about Wisconsin, I set about researching different nature areas, parks, mountains, lakes, rivers, and activities we could experience as a family. It took a long time to build an itinerary for the trip, hours of going from site to site looking at maps and figuring out what there was to do, where to stay and eat, and how to get there. When we finally got there, the beauty of the area took our breath away.

So after all that work, including how it paid off, the idea hit me like a hurricane. What if there was a website that could simplify planning a nature adventure trip? What if you could just type in the location and the activity you like and be presented with a list of options—a list of places to go and things to do, complete with how to get there, where to stay and eat? It would open the door to a whole new way of travel. The idea kept shaping in my head, and I wrote the business plan on the plane ride back. Now I had an idea and found myself excited and full of energy to execute.

I set about building a startup focused on traveling and discovering nature from the ground up. I applied and was accepted to the Startup Leadership Program (SLP) and learned how to build a startup, which included, the process and resources needed to do so. All of a sudden, I had drive. I was still working full time during the day and spent evenings and weekends working on my startup. After six months of doing both, I finally quit my corporate job and set about working on my startup full time. I was forty-nine years old. I realized how happy it made me to work on what I love. It didn't feel like work. Our home life improved drastically, too. Happy mom, happy house.

I entered my fifties with a new sense of purpose and joy, and all it took was a change of mindset. I was pursuing my interests and planning my life with personal and career goals combined. My work took me to places I'd never dreamed of going. I met a whole new sector of society in the startup world that I would never have met otherwise. Innovative people with amazing drive and resilience. I now have new friends who inspire and guide me every day. I'm seeing the world in a whole new way. I learned that you only get by giving. All kinds of doors opened up to me when I volunteered to become the SLP Program Lead and to help another twenty-five leaders find their way in the startup world.

My startup took my family and me to many of the beautiful national parks in the United States. My travels were now for "research." I remember standing by Phelps Lake in Grand Teton National Park, after hiking for miles in the wilderness with my best friend, watching the exotic birds that travel to the area every summer, and really experiencing joy and stillness.

What I wish I had known . . . and what my advice is to you, the reader

My philosophy is to keep moving—to move and push beyond what I ever thought possible, physically and mentally, and to challenge myself to enter uncharted territories, ever learning along the way, but always connecting to that stillness within. Embrace the joy that only comes from being ever so grateful. At fifty-one, I can honestly say that I'm happier now than I've ever been. I'm working at what I love and not stressing about money.

My life experiences so far have taken me up and down so many times. My forties brought lots of struggles and challenges, but also a positive turn. I persevered through chronic pain with help of new methodologies and connecting with the balance of body and mind. I was always learning new ways and having new ideas. Every time I fall, I find a way to get back up. The joy of life, enjoying every day to the fullest, seeing my girls grow, and more important, being there for them, and exploring of the world around us continue for me. I'm sure there'll be ups and downs yet to come, but I embrace the hardships that make the ups that much more enjoyable.

TRUST YOUR GUT

Me before Forty

If I say, "My hometown was so small," you would think I was starting to tell you a joke, right? But seriously, my hometown was so small that I could stand on the street corner downtown and know every person who passed me—whether they were on foot, bike, or in a car! I was the youngest of six and raised in the Midwest. I experienced a typical Midwestern upbringing. We were a white, Irish Catholic, lower-middle-class family smack dab in the middle of a predominantly German Protestant town. Not much drama came our way, and we lived happily most days.

As a child, I attended the local Catholic grade school along with kids from all of the neighboring towns and cities, however, no one was local. I was too young to truly understand how deeply our city was immersed in the Methodist, Presbyterian, and Baptist religions. My siblings and I were a part of a small faction of Catholics, but I was oblivious to this fact. When it came time to choose a high school, I desperately wanted to go to school with my neighborhood friends, who, of course, were Protestant! But really, what I wanted was to blend in. When I started high school, the overachiever in me emerged, and I overcame some of the insecurities I'd experienced from being teased at a younger age for being what the other kids called "fat." Looking back at pictures from my childhood, I am surprised by the teasing, because I wasn't truly fat in the traditional sense of the word. I was actually a pretty standard build. I never could determine the root of the teasing other than the fact that most children try to see what insults trigger a reaction and build on them. Not only did I want to be with my friends, but I wanted them to think I was amazing! I was a swimmer, softball player, varsity cheerleading captain, National Honor Society member, consistent honor roll recipient, and class leader. Regardless of all of my accomplishments, I never felt successful or like I belonged. When I was sixteen, my father passed away after a long fight with cancer. My world turned upside down and never quite righted itself again. Everything I understood to be normal was gone. I had gone from being my mother's child to being her peer. I no longer had anyone to truly lean on, confide in, or go to in times of trouble. Instead, I was the one providing comfort, stability, and love. Unfortunately, at that time, therapy was not the norm. People only sought professional help if they were "crazy." I wasn't crazy—just incredibly sad and lonely. I had no answers, so I put my head down and worked hard in school. I stayed out of trouble, got a job, and made my own money. The last thing I wanted to do was cause my mom any problems. I never wanted to be the cause of her sadness or anger. I guess I was living the life I thought I should and not my authentic one.

I went from a childhood of always being teased for being fat to becoming a teen who wanted to overcome my childhood challenges, and then to a twenty-something still feeling the same way. Unfortunately, it seems that at each life milestone, I would look back and realize I wasn't quite perfect, but not nearly as bad as I had remembered. In retrospect, I wish I could have those days back to appreciate my mind, body, and spirit in the moment.

As I was fast approaching my fortieth birthday, I found myself living in a city that had become my adoptive home—as I hadn't lived in my home-town for more than twenty-two years. That is the mark of claiming a new town as home, right? Living there more than half your life? I had my husband's large immediate family and enormous extended family with whom I spent more time than I did my own. I had been, at that point, married for thirteen years and a mother to three children, twelve, ten, and six years old. My life was the typical chaos you'd expect, with laundry piles, homework deadlines, basketball practice, and science projects. My husband, a wonderful man, was the financial supporter and disciplinarian but left the lion's share of everything else to me. Because I'd been raised in a household that preached, "You can handle anything" and "*We* never quit anything,"

I thought my overwhelming fatigue was normal. I felt my deep sadness and severe sensitivity were reasonable. But as my hair started to thin and I couldn't make it through the day without a two-hour nap (and that's after an eight-hour night's sleep), I began to suspect something was going awry. In addition to the fatigue, sadness, and thinning hair, I was easily irritated. The littlest thing set me off. I'm sure my poor family felt as if they were living on a minefield. One false move and "thar she blows!" My body seemed to be betraying me at every turn. My joints were painful and swollen. I walked like an elderly woman so I was convinced this was the early onset of rheumatoid arthritis because the autoimmune disorder ran—no *raced*—through my family gene pool.

My Emotional and Physical Journey Post-Forty

With all that was happening, I was quickly approaching middle age. Argh! This was the ideal time to fall victim to the disease. But I still did nothing about it because that's what moms do. We are the proverbial shoemaker. We make shoes for everyone else before we ever consider making our own. So I continued to ignore my symptoms, one by one, finding an excuse for each. Cold, colorless toes and fingertips were just bad circulation resulting from a traditional Midwestern winter. My legs looked like I was wearing fishnet stockings but, in reality, I was looking at my blood vessels through my skin. I explained it as simply the result of no sun exposure. Weakness in my hands? Well, I don't have time to work out. Everything is weak at this point! Red butterfly shaped rash on my face? Doesn't everyone experience a little bit of rosacea now and then? Slap on some thick makeup, and we're good to go. The desperate feelings of helplessness, sadness, anxiety, and lack of interest in anyone or anything should have sent me running to the nearest emergency room. But there was absolutely, positively, no way I was going to admit to depression. We are *not* crazy in our house! No mental illness here. No way, no how. It's just a bad day. Suck it up, Buttercup. You'll be fine.

I wasn't fine. I was sick and tired of being sick and tired. One morning, I simply woke up and made a call to my OB/GYN because I had no general practitioner. She recommended I contact a doctor she knew who specialized in internal medicine. Thus began my journey of being poked and prodded. Doctors began trying to rule everything out because they couldn't put their finger on the root of the problem. Did I have chronic fatigue syndrome? Had I been bitten by a tick and contracted Lyme disease? Sjogren's syndrome? Was I clinically depressed? No, I was suffering from lupus. After a year and a half of ruling illnesses out, the doctors settled on their diagnosis. Over the next ten years, the symptoms continued to come and go. Sometimes, it was debilitating. Other times it was tolerable. Now it seems to be in remission, and life is manageable

As a little girl, I had dreamed of being a famous morning show anchor. I was sure I was going to be the next Jane Pauley or Katie Couric. I worked hard to receive a journalism degree from a local college and worked a few years to get some experience under my belt. However, somewhere along the way I married and had children. So one year became five which became twenty and, in reality, all I had become was a housewife who had not worked since 2001. I was a stay-at-home mom with no real money of my own. When I needed money for groceries or school clothes, I went to my husband and felt like a child asking my dad for an allowance. In my husband's defense, I was in an old-school relationship and he earned the money, I didn't. This lack of independence didn't afford me many opportunities with my kids. I had to get creative with my entertainment. Unfortunately, struggling financially stripped me of my self-confidence and was the start of a truly dark time. I was living in an adopted city, surrounded by his family. My closest relative was four hours away. I had no support and no friends. I began to submerge myself in my children and take on their triumphs and sorrows. People say, "You are only as happy as your saddest child." With three children to create opportunities for sadness, I spent a great deal of time in the doldrums. I was losing my sense of self. I had no personal interests and nothing to call my own.

At this point in time, I was moving through life on autopilot. I was empty. I wasn't happy, and I wasn't sad. I was uninspired and looking for some sort of spark. Even though I knew I was truly blessed, I saw that I needed to appreciate more, live more, love more, touch more. I needed to find true sincerity in myself, a feeling of wholeness and peace. I had to rid myself of this burden of self-doubt and stand on my own two feet, supporting myself. What do I want to be when I grow up? How can I work and make money while continuing to be a good mother and wife? I was paralyzed with fear. At the age of 45, I asked myself, *God, what is your purpose for me? What has my life stood for? What does it stand for now?* I was asking for help, any sign of guidance, a whisper. I began to worry that I would be a person who exited the world without knowing why I had entered it.

So I started working on myself. Up to this point, I had found excuse after excuse as to why I was failing. Art Linkletter once said, "Things turn out best for people who make the best of how things turn out." You know? He's right. As humans, we forget that we have an unbelievable control over our own destiny. I began to work daily to be an authentic representation of the woman staring back at me in the mirror. I knew it was not going to happen overnight and I knew I needed help getting there.

In 2008, I experienced a paradigm shift of epic proportions. I saw my life take a turn as two very important things came into focus: an inner spirituality and an inner-city school. At this time, my oldest son was beginning his high school career attending a private religious school. One day, as I was wandering on campus, I came across a flyer for a multi-week retreat for spiritual guidance. It was exactly what I needed. The retreat gave me the gift of weeks of introspection, and I began to find bits of myself. I realized everything in my life was a gift in some way, shape or form. I set out to live my life with those words in mind and begin my quest to find the next right step. Someone once said, "Never fear shadows. They simply mean there is a light shining somewhere nearby."

At the same time I was rediscovering myself, I decided to dip my toe back into the employment pool, but I had absolutely no idea how to go about it. I was paralyzed with fear. As a child, I hadn't been encouraged to ask for help. A person appears stronger if they are able to figure things out on their own. But as I grew, I discovered that worrying wasn't going to get me a job and that asking for help was actually a sign of strength. So I took a deep breath and picked up the phone. On the other end of the phone, a friend answered. Choking back tears of anxiety and fear, I asked her if I could come to her office to talk. She kindly accepted my request and I rushed right over. As I sat at her boardroom table in tears, I spoke loudly, irrationally and, I'm sure, incoherently about how I lacked any marketable skills and there was no way anyone would ever hire me. After all, I had received a journalism degree in college and never used it afterward. Throughout my marriage, I had been a part-time sales representative marketing everything from copiers to radio advertising, and failing abysmally, I might add. I had been a part-time travel agent, telemarketer for an insurance company, and furniture salesperson—anything I could do to somehow contribute to the family's bottom line while still eking out enough time to do the laundry, go to the grocery store, help with homework, chauffeur kids to practices, make dinner—you get the picture. But not one job prepared me for having a career in a field I loved. Not one job gave me the experience I needed to get hired after many years out of the workforce. I was doomed. I only knew who I thought I was supposed to be and not who I was. These two are very different people.

But my friend had a great idea. She happened to be on the board of directors for a new and innovative inner-city high school. If I would be willing to start as a volunteer wherever they needed me for a few hours a week, I could get my foot in the door and see what else became available down the line. Because the school was just getting established, the administration was more likely to give someone a chance without the work experience required for a particular job. I thought this was the perfect opportunity to find my way back into the workforce.

I took my friend up on the offer to introduce me to the vice-president of the school and, within days, I was in the middle of my first real interview in more than a decade. Driving down to the school, I was a complete wreck. I was navigating through under-resourced neighborhood streets I had never driven in my life. I was sweating through my outdated suit, and my heart was beating through my chest. I arrived at the school and found my way to the office. After a few minutes of pleasant small talk, I finally relaxed and was offered the volunteer position. For several weeks, I spent time in every aspect of the school. No job was too lowly. I made copies for teachers. I filed and organized offices for administration. I worked in the cafeteria. I learned quickly and worked hard. Within a short time, I was offered a position to put my writing skills to good use in a job I had never known existed or considered for myself. At that moment in time, at the age of forty-four, I was embarking on my first true career—as a grant writer, raising funds for families who otherwise would be unable to send their children to a college preparatory school and giving them hope of continuing on to college to earn a degree.

My newfound employment made me feel like a grown up again! I was exchanging my old vocabulary of words such as *wow* and *very* for new words like *magnificent* and *exceedingly*. I began to see hope and watched my self-worth grow. Not that supporting my husband and raising my children weren't fulfilling, don't get me wrong. But I was starting to find myself again through my writing. I was making a difference outside my home, and it was a big difference. Up to that point, my greatest fear had been not having enough to fill in the dash between the date of my birth and death. I think someone once called it "living your dash." I wanted people to recall more than the fact that I was a mom and a wife.

As I began to hit my stride as a contributing member of society, my body began to defy me again. But this time around, lupus was only one of the culprits. I, like many other middle-aged women, was staring perimenopause directly in the face. It started with hot flash after hot flash, often sending me reeling outdoors for relief. My son described me as resembling the inflatable tube man at the local car dealership. Night sweats slowly made their way into my life, which gave way to insomnia, which, in turn, led to fatigue. Covers on, covers off, covers on. . . . My periods began to change and eventually stopped. Unfortunately, I still experienced all of the other symptoms of menstruating: anxiety with a racing heart, mood swings, and depression. I was quickly and inexplicably gaining weight and losing confidence. I was zeroing in on full blown menopause.

I had an idea of what might be happening to me, but I wasn't completely sure. My mom never went through traditional menopause as the result of a radical hysterectomy in her late thirties. Even if she had gone through menopause, she would never have made it apparent to the family. She wasn't one to complain or share her pain partly because of how she was raised as well as the generation from which she came. I have an older sister who, although three years older than I, was no better informed and no further along in the process. So I entered this phase of my life blindly, armed only with a search engine to find answers.

One day as I was getting my hair cut, I was speaking generally with the stylist about how I was feeling and what I was experiencing. She knew my background with the lupus issue and suggested I look outside of the traditional medicine route to find relief. At this point, I was willing to try anything to feel better. So I took her up on her advice and made a phone call to a local holistic physician she recommended. This particular doctor developed craniosacral therapy and used Oriental medicine in his private practice. He started studying this unique form of medicine in the early 1970s in Japan, China, Hong Kong, and Taiwan. His studies continue today, and he lectures at the college and graduate levels as well as at national and international conferences on health. My family still jokingly refers to him as my "voodoo" doctor. But of course, we always make fun of the things we don't understand.

When I called to set my appointment with the doctor, he was booked for the next six months. I picked my date, then hung up the phone and cried. I wanted more than anything to feel better and now I had to wait six long months. In the meantime, I had read somewhere that exercise was one of the keys to staving off the effects of menopause. Up to this point, I had only participated in organized sports for fun and socialization. I didn't particularly care to exercise on my own for the health of it. Plus, I was still in a situation where I didn't feel comfortable dropping $100 a month on a gym membership. Just then, I passed my closet and looked in. What I saw was a pair of tennis shoes and right then decided to give a very inexpensive option, running, a try. And run I did. I was no Forrest Gump, but I ran. I started to slowly and methodically build my confidence and stamina. After months of jogging, I entered my first 5K race. Now, I'm not going to give you my race time but, suffice it to say, I finished, and I was not the last person to cross the finish line. A success! Those articles I read were right. I felt better and I was starting to do something for myself. I went on to run a few more 5ks and a 10k. I even trained for a half marathon until I suffered a hip fracture. I think this was my cue to go back to the real reasons I was running: to feel better and keep a clear head. To this day, I continue to run a few days a week for those very reasons.

The doctor's appointment finally came, and I am grateful it did. I spent an hour that day and several appointments that year with the doctor as he introduced a series of healing procedures: bone setting, acupuncture, craniosacral therapy (a hands-on approach to release tensions deep in the body, relieving pain and dysfunction and improving whole-body health and performance), visceral manipulation (another hands-on approach to move and release fascial restrictions in the abdomen and pelvis to encourage the normal movement and function of your internal organs), applied kinesiology muscle testing, Neuro-Emotional Technique (a psycho-emotional therapy based on the physiological foundations of stress-related responses), and Contact Reflex Analysis (a technique that analyzes the energy that flows through every organ, gland, and cell in the body). A shift in muscle response is used as an indicator of energy balance or imbalance in a particular area and Neurolink, a system of health care that uses the brain to optimize the function and repair of the body. Using these techniques combined with my exercise regime and the addition of health supplements and vitamins, I began to feel relief. The doctor helped me to realize my body was an engine that needed to be treated as such. It needed to be maintained regularly and provided the best fuel to make it perform at its maximum capacity.

For several years now, as I approach fifty-three, I have been visiting the "voodoo" doctor annually, loving my family, eating healthy, running weekly, and staying true to my spirituality. I have even added a daily sunrise hot yoga practice, beginner guitar lessons, and writing a children's story to my repertoire. You know, the answer seems so simple. But I truly feel better than I ever have in my life. Unfortunately, I think I have a few more years to battle menopause. You know what? Bring it on!

What would I tell my younger self or someone who may be just discovering she has lupus and entering menopause? How do the two impact each other? Advice about not forgetting yourself in love for family?

If I could take a trip back and have a glass of wine with my younger self, I would hold her hand tightly and tell her to trust her gut. I would tell her that when her body, heart, spirit, or mind tells her something, believe it. Don't ignore it. I would rather be thought of as a hypochondriac than someone who nearly wasted fifteen valuable years of her life.

Had I trusted myself, I could have entered menopause with a healthier mind and body. Instead of battling the symptoms of two afflictions at once, I could have handled them one at a time. Some of the issues of both mimic each other closely and I believe were almost doubled because of the combination of experiencing both at the same time.

Lupus, and really all autoimmune disorders are sneaky. They don't present themselves in our bodies the way traditional illnesses do, which makes them difficult to diagnose. If you think something is wrong, pursue it with fervor. And if one doctor doesn't find it, consult with another . . . and another, until you have found your answer.

But most importantly, I'd leave my younger self with this thought: practice self-love. We all know that *we can't give to others what we don't understand ourselves.* Take time out to take care of yourself, regardless of how selfish or unnatural it feels. In the end, you will be a better parent, spouse, employee, child, and friend. And you will teach your children a valuable lesson as well.

GOD BY MY SIDE

Me before Forty

I grew up as an only child in San Diego, California. I had a great childhood, surrounded by many cousins and friends. My parents were very faithful believers in God and studied the Bible any chance they could. I spent most of my weekends at church, attending on both Saturdays and Sundays. My parents separated when I was a toddler and lived in separate homes; however, they ensured that I had everything I needed. As an assistant pastor, my father took me to church with him on Sundays, which would last from morning until the early evening. As a young child, it was hard for me to stay focused on the church sermons. I spent most of my time in church doodling or moving from aisle to aisle while my father stood at the podium with the other pastors preaching. I didn't understand why we went to church so often or why I had to sit there for endless hours at a time, but as I got older, I began to understand why my parents wanted me rooted in the church, and how loving God would make me the strongest person I never knew I could be.

I was a very shy child growing up, and I didn't make many friends in grade school. I never really fit into groups in grade school and often ate lunch alone. Where I grew up, you either hung out with the Black crowd or the Filipino crowd. There was no mixing of ethnicities until I got to high school. I made a few friends in the tenth grade in my driver's education class, with whom I am still dear friends today, twenty-eight years later. I have always been a perfectionist by nature and was known as the "good" girl who never got into any trouble. Instead, in my free time, I stayed in my room where I focused my attention on my passions of painting, drawing, and writing. My friends had to practically beg me to go out with them on the weekends, because all I wanted to do was paint, draw, and write.

My parents separated when I was two years old. My mother started dating another man when I was eleven years old, who embraced me completely and opened a new door of adventure for myself and my mother. Many of the things I witnessed as a child kept me introverted until I got into my adolescent years. During my junior year of high school, my stepfather was involved in a workplace violence incident. Our world was completely turned upside down, and our lives were never the same. One day my mother and I were living in a peaceful loving home, and within three days, we were forced to temporarily move into a relative's two-bedroom apartment. To see an incident in the news headlines that involved someone so close to me was mind-boggling. I couldn't wrap my brain around the thought of this incident being our new reality. How could someone I'd loved and trusted for six years do something like this? Where would we live? How would this incident impact our lives going forward? Would we have to testify in court? From that day forward, the many fears from my childhood that haunted me only intensified because of the incident with my stepfather.

Despite the pain of losing my stepfather to a life sentence in prison and starting a new life in another home with just me and my mother, I somehow made it through high school and managed to land straight A's. I drowned myself in my studies, perhaps as a way to cope with such a traumatizing situation. I don't understand how I remained focused after experiencing such turmoil and living in constant fear, but I knew that I wanted to be successful . Even as a young child, I felt driven to succeed.

My stepfather's imprisonment was just one of many significant events that happened in my life that shaped the person I am today. Despite the difficulties, I graduated from high school with honors, went on to receive a bachelor's degree in criminology and criminal justice, a master's degree in business, and a paralegal certification in business litigation. Despite graduating from school with honors, and at the top of my class, I had a very slow but ultimately successful career path.

I soon discovered that the foundation built by my parents of loving and trusting in God would carry me through the painful and difficult times, making me less fearful and more God-fearing throughout my life.

I knew that I wanted to be successful since I was a young child, but how would I get there if I lived in constant fear, regardless of how well I did in school? How would I excel in life without facing a few bumps in the road and learning a few lessons along the way? I spent most of my life pleasing others, even if it meant sacrificing my own needs, feelings, and time. I always feared that saying no would lead to a conflict that I have always feared. I wanted to be accepted by others, having that unconscious fear of being left alone.

Because both of my parents were strong believers in God, I was aware of God's existence; however, as I progressed into my adult life, I did not fully understand what believing in him and serving him meant. I began to attend church more regularly on my own, due to my own curiosity of finding out what it meant to truly love and accept God as my personal savior.

As I got through college, I became quite close to a cousin who was a very strong believer in God. Her love for God really opened my eyes to what it meant to have faith and to love the Lord unconditionally, despite the losses and pain she endured in her life. When she moved, I felt an emptiness, but she planted a seed in me before she boarded the airplane. Being the fearful women that we were, my mom and I asked her, "Aren't you afraid to fly?" She looked back at me before she boarded (this was when non-passengers were still allowed to go to the gates) and said, "The only thing I fear is God." Although I didn't understand that statement at the time, her words stuck with me forever.

After my cousin left, I visited a few college events on campus and I even attempted to get baptized at a church that we attended together, however, I still didn't get that "feeling" that my parents and my cousin always spoke of. What did it feel like to truly love God? To have faith in God, even in the midst of our most difficult and trying times? I was curious to find out.

Regardless of my desire to find faith in God, my attendance in church slowly diminished due to homework, internships, and work. One day I was driving home from school, and the Holy Spirit of God completely took over my soul. I was listening to a CD by Mary J. Blige, called "My Life." The interlude was playing, which had sounds of a door cracking open. In my mind, when I heard the interlude, I pictured a door to a dark room opening, and the light of Jesus Christ shining through it as it opened wider. The words of the interlude read:

> *Oh, oh thank you thank you*
>
> *Oh this is my life (this is my life)*
>
> *You are my life (you are my life)*
>
> *You are my life*
>
> *And I thank you (I wanna thank you)*
>
> *Oh I thank you (I wanna thank you)*
>
> *I thank you for blessing me.*

When I heard the words "I thank you for blessing me," I began sobbing hysterically and I couldn't figure out why. But they weren't tears of sadness, but tears of joy. I finally felt the presence of God, a deep, secure, nurturing, trusting feeling that I had never felt before. God was preparing me for my father's death, something that I was expecting due his cancer diagnosis several months earlier.

I lost my father shortly after I completed my second advanced degree, at age twenty-five. At that time, it seemed like my entire world had crumbled. It seemed as though I had lost everything. I lost my father, my job, my mom lost her job, and I broke up with my fiancé all within a few weeks. As hard as it was to digest these losses, through it all, I found a calming peace. My entire life I was always so afraid of the unknown, being alone or losing someone or something that I cherished most. But finding God gave me an inner peace and security. God helped me to have trust and to step out on faith.

Be strong and courageous. Do not be afraid or terrified because of them, for the Lord your God goes with you; he will never leave you nor forsake you. Deuteronomy 31:6

Although I grieved relentlessly over my father, having God on my side and carrying me through one of the most difficult times of my life brought me closer to HIM. I frequently questioned why God left me alone. How could this happen to me? How could God leave me all alone when HE promised to never leave or forsake me? I soon realized that God never left me, and that he was there with me through it all—the good, the bad, and the most trying times of my life. He always protected me and never left or forsaken me.

Although I was a work in progress, after I truly found God, the fear of being alone, judged, not loved, not good enough didn't haunt me the way it did growing up. When I found myself down, out and fearful, there was an inner voice from God that was always there within me that carried me through my pains, sufferings, and fears.

I met my husband eighteen years ago, and we have been married for over eleven years. My husband and I didn't want children immediately after we were married so we would be able enjoy one another and travel. We started trying to conceive after two years of marriage. I stopped taking birth control pills when we were ready to start trying in January 2008, thinking that within three to six months, I would conceive. Every month, there was no positive result. I began to worry as my age was starting to advance. I was now thirty-three and I still didn't have my first child.

My doctor ran a few blood tests and determined that I had a hypothyroid. My thyroid levels were slightly low, which threw off my follicle stimulating hormone. I was prescribed a small dose of medication to treat my thyroid hormone, which would in term treat the follicle stimulating hormone. My doctor also informed me that we had to be actively trying to conceive for one full year before being referred to an infertility specialist.

My husband and I continued trying to conceive with no luck. I was now thirty-four, and I began to worry that maybe I would have early menopause, which may be contributing to my infertility. After a full year of officially trying to conceive, my doctor referred me to an infertility clinic. There were numerous classes and tests that we had to undertake before being provided a treatment plan. One of the first procedures was an initial sonogram to detect whether the thyroid medication that I was prescribed helped me to produce follicles. Once the doctor determined that I had follicles in both ovaries, I was referred to the lab where they placed dye in my uterus to determine whether there was a blockage in my fallopian tubes. There were numerous other tests to determine my hormone levels and to determine whether there was any family history of certain illnesses that may cause infertility. My husband also had to undergo a few blood tests as well and provide semen samples.

After a few months, my doctor determined that I had an unexplained infertility. My husband however, had no infertility issues, and his sperm count came back well above average.

Due to my advanced age, my infertility doctor placed me on Clomid, an oral medication that can be used to stimulate ovulation.

As we were undergoing treatment and infertility education, emotional part of trying to conceive began to take its toll on me physically and emotionally. I found myself thinking about conceiving 24 hours a day, 7 days a week. Every month during ovulation, I was excited to conceive and thought that each time I had sexual intercourse with my husband, I would become pregnant. Finally, after three rounds of Clomid and two unsuccessful intrauterine inseminations, my husband and I took a month off from the infertility treatment to refocus and enjoy one another. I was also in the middle of a career transition, which I needed to focus on.

A good friend of mine suggested that I try acupuncture to conceive. I didn't think anything of it and actually gave up the idea of becoming pregnant at that point.

At this point, my husband and I even talked to a few other friends about the adoption and foster home process. We accepted the fact that we were not going to have children, and that we could possibly give a child a loving home who really needed it by adoption or fostering.

One day during the Thanksgiving holiday, I did some research on infertility acupuncture clinics in San Diego. I found a clinic that was the one for me. I called and made an appointment at the beginning of December 2011.

After discovering the infertility acupuncture clinic, my husband and I decided to get another treatment of the intrauterine insemination.

On December 30, 2011, my husband and I were packing to spend the New Year's Eve weekend at Disneyland. We had an appointment for an intrauterine insemination at one o'clock and had to carry the fresh sperm that my husband injected into a sealed container between my breasts to keep it warm. The drive was about 25 minutes away from home, which was quite nerve wrecking. When we arrived at the clinic for our third intrauterine insemination, I didn't know what to expect. I had it in my mind that I wouldn't conceive, not because I didn't want to, but because I had finally come to a point in my life where I figured it probably would not happen. As I lay on the clinic bed, my doctor closely monitored my follicles; she told me that I only had one large and very ripe follicle that was ready to burst any day. I felt my heart sink. How would we conceive with only one follicle? I just knew this intrauterine insemination would be unsuccessful.

Later, on December 31, 2011, while my husband and I were at Disneyland, we threw a penny into the pond next to the haunted mansion and prayed for conception. A few weeks later, on January 16, 2012, after forgetting about the entire procedure and nearly forgetting to take a pregnancy test, I found out that I was pregnant with our sweet baby girl.

I got pregnant with my daughter at the age of thirty-six. I experienced a hard pregnancy due to hyperemesis gravidarum. The symptoms can include extreme nausea and vomiting, as well as rapid weight loss, dehydration, electrolyte imbalance, dizziness, and excessive saliva. Hyperemesis gravidarum affects as many as 3 percent of pregnancies, leading to over 167,000 emergency room visits each year in the US.

Due to my condition, I was unable to do anything physically or mentally. My husband and I grew very close when we were trying to conceive, but after being diagnosed with hyperemesis gravidarum, our marriage and sexual life suffered. I was also unable to go to work, see friends, attend birthday parties, or attend church. I was locked in my bedroom all day and night for almost two months. The only time that I saw daylight was when I went to and from the hospital.

Having hyperemesis gravidarum was a very dark and depressing time in my life. During that phase of my life, I felt the most depressed than I've ever felt. I could not hold any food in my system for almost fourteen weeks. I had many visits to the emergency room, along with being hospitalized for a period of time to receive IV fluid treatments every few days for my condition and for extreme dehydration.

At home, everything smelled bad and triggered my illness. My mother prepared a very bland range of food for me, to limit the smells that triggered my illness. We had to rid our home of many fragrances that made me ill as well. My mother, husband, and even my dog had a hard time witnessing me go through so much turmoil. My husband and I thought about terminating the pregnancy if my condition worsened. In a survey of over eight hundred women with hyperemesis gravidarum, more than one in seven women with the disorder decided to terminate the pregnancy, primarily because they had no hope for relief from the condition.

As the weeks went by, I was finally able to hold food down a bit more. Going to the hospital regularly to receive fluids and vitamins intravenously helped tremendously. No one can tell you what it is like to experience hyperemesis gravidarum, but I can tell you from my experience that there is light at the end of the tunnel. My advice: do not terminate your pregnancy! The illness will get better with time and medication. Seek help early and do not be afraid to take medications prescribed by your doctor. These medications are designed to treat cancer patients with nausea and will not harm your baby.

At twenty weeks, I was finally able to enjoy my pregnancy, my friends and family, and return to work. Most important, I was able to eat again and bond with my growing baby. When I felt every kick, hiccup, movement, and saw every sonogram from each doctor's visit, I could not imagine my life without our precious baby girl.

My Journey Post-Forty

By the time I went back to work after having my daughter, I had lost most of my baby weight, with maybe five pounds left to lose. I was a bit surprised at how fast I fit back into my work clothes. I had no idea that I was about to embark on a physical change that I wasn't aware of until I turned forty.

On May 15, 2015, I was diagnosed with Graves' disease, which causes a swelling of the neck and protrusion of the eyes resulting from an overactive thyroid gland. I noticed that I continued losing weight long after I gave birth to my daughter in 2012, which was very rapid and continued even with minimal exercise. I was ten pounds below my normal weight after having my daughter two years prior. My eyes were also bulging, which is another trait of an over active thyroid and Graves disease. After becoming concerned with my bulging eyes and rapid weight loss, my primary care physician referred me to an endocrinologist who informed me that I would not be able to conceive and would need to be on medication for two years to treat my overactive thyroid. I was devastated knowing that I had to be on medication and that I probably would not be able to conceive again. At this time, I was already heading into my forties, so having a baby after that timeframe just didn't seem possible.

When I was diagnosed with Graves' disease, I had to undergo more testing and blood tests to determine what type of treatment I needed. My doctor placed me on methimazole, which is used to treat hyperthyroidism. If untreated, Graves' disease could also cause double vision, changes in the shape of the eye muscles, and even blindness.

After being on methimazole for over a year, I was able to get off of the medication completely. I found holistic ways to eliminate thyroid toxins through a very trusted source. I changed my diet and cut out any dietary hazards that elevated my thyroid levels. I began taking natural herbs and I eliminated thyroid toxic substances from my diet. My protocol also consisted of adopting a Paleolithic diet, and practicing dietary allergy elimination and nutritional supplementation. As part of a holistic protocol, stress reduction is also paramount.

Turning forty felt like a skin peel. I finally felt like I knew who I was. I feared growing "old" for so long, but when I turned forty, I felt like it was my new twenties. I was a homeowner for the third time, married for nine years, had a beautiful baby girl, was at the peak of my career, and had finally made it above the six-figure salary mark. At the age of forty, walls were being torn down, barriers were being destroyed, and doors were opening. The confidence that I lacked in my younger years suddenly appeared. I finally felt I was in a good place mentally and physically.

As I began a new journey in finding myself, I sought my personal interests again, such as painting, drawing, and writing. As my daughter grew into a toddler and then into a more independent young girl, my fears of letting go began to slowly diminish, and I was able to focus on myself and my own personal interests.

How did your experiences affect how you live your life now?

I believe my past experiences have shaped the person I am today. I still have fears, especially being a mother to a young child, but I know I can look to God for support when I have any fear or doubt. Throughout all of the experiences in my life, the good, the bad, the traumatizing, the hurtful, the rewarding, and the happiest, I believe that I can walk through it as long as I have God by my side.

When I find myself fearing and in doubt, I refer to my favorite Bible verses:

> *With God, all things are possible.* (Matthew 19:26)

> *Be strong and of good courage, do not fear nor be afraid of them; for the Lord your God, He is the One who goes with you. He will not leave you nor forsake you.* (Deuteronomy 31:6)

To help me cope through difficult times, I always read my favorite poem called "Footprints in the Sand" by Mary Stevenson. This poem gives me the reassurance that God will carry me through anything and help me withstand the burdens I can't handle on my own.

After I lost my father, my life actually changed for the better, because I no longer had to settle for anything, and I discovered my own self-worth. I felt a sense of security that God was always walking by my side. God never promised that I would not face difficult times in life, but he did promise to carry me through them.

What are your greatest fears and how do you overcome those?

Before I turned forty, I lived in with fear. Although I was brought up in a very loving home, fear seemed like second nature growing up. I feared everything as a child from the hot water heater exploding in the laundry room next door to our apartment; to accidents happening by car, train, boat or plane; or losing loved ones to illnesses and death. As an adult, I feared being judged, voicing my opinion to avoid conflicts, standing up for myself, being left alone, and taking my career to the next level.

How have you dealt with perimenopause and/or menopause?

As a woman in her early forties, I have experienced some changes in my body such as decreasing fertility; however, I have not officially been diagnosed as a perimenopausal patient.

The physical changes in my body at this phase of my life have actually impacted my marriage and other aspects of my life in a positive way. My overactive thyroid is now under control and I feel healthier than I've ever felt. I exercise four or five times a week and feel fit. I am no longer on any medications and will continue my dietary path to stay in good physical shape.

What was going on in your life after your forties that inspired you to bring a new perspective (promise of life) into existence? Why?

In my twenties, I took everything personally, constantly jumping on the defense about issues that were so irrelevant, and I felt compelled to change jobs to get ahead or promoted. Part of that behavior stemmed from my fear of being judged by others. Further, due to the financial strains that my mother and I faced after the incident with my stepfather, I became a depressed, bitter, and envious person, especially over my friends' successes, because I felt that I deserved to have a great career due to all of my schooling and academic achievements. Instead, I found myself constantly getting passed over for promotions and jobs. I suffered from workplace bullying, harassment, discrimination, gender inequality, and racism during my early career in the legal field. I was too afraid to speak up and defend myself when those issues arose. It took much inner growth and letting go of my fears to move up the corporate ladder. In my mental state today as a forty-two-year-old woman, I have no problem addressing these issues and defending myself in the workplace, or in any situation for that matter.

Between the ages of thirty-eight and forty, I felt the most confident in almost everything that I had feared or doubted. In my previous employment, I was blessed enough to work for two leaders who were extremely brilliant and feared nothing. They mentored me in my career development and helped me to face my fears. My leader at the time conveyed a message to me that I carried to my next employer: "All you have to do is talk. Provide a high-level summary of the topic, and just be yourself. Let your knowledge do the talking."

As I grew into my forties, I became less worried about the inevitable and more confident in myself. Although I am still a work in progress, I've learned to value my self-worth and slowly let down those barriers of fear.

Today, I am working in a career that I strived so hard to achieve. It is not easy being a woman of color in corporate America, however, God equipped me at each job, whether it was a good or bad experience, to learn something. I finally feel like I am in control of my life. Thanks to help from my life experiences, mentors, and my husband of eleven years, I face challenges without worrying about what is, what was, or what should be. My husband taught me to be fearless. The little things that got me down thirty years ago don't have an impact on me today.

What I wish I had known . . . and what my advice is to you, the reader

For anyone suffering from Graves' disease or hyperemesis gravidarum, I would like to provide some advice on proactive steps that you can take to get both diseases under control.

Graves' Disease

Below is a list of thyroid toxic substances that should be eliminated from a hyperthyroid diet:

- Soy

- Goitrogens (a thyroid antagonist found in food) such as

    - Cabbage

    - Turnips

    - Kale

    - Rutabaga

    - Watercress

    - Brussels sprouts

    - Cauliflower

    - Broccoli

    - Kohlrabi

Returning to a Paleolithic diet that is made of meat, nuts, and produce may remove one of the main offending causes behind autoimmune problems.

Below is a list of supplements that I have used to treat hyperthyroidism:

- Foundation Formula 1 tablet, twice daily

- Acidophilus and bifidobacteria as directed

- EPA/DHA 3,000 mg and higher

- L-carnitine 2 to 4 grams per day

- Glutamine 2 grams, upon arising

- GLA 300 2 capsules, with each meal

- Flaxseed oil 2 tablespoons

- Vitamin C Ester-C (500 mg), three times per day

- Vitamin E 400 IU

- Magnesium 400-800 mg (slow mag may be needed)

Use the following ingredients when making detox shakes:

- Turmeric

- Garlic

- Ginger

- Reishi or ganoderma

- 1 tsp of almond butter

- 1 scoop of Genesis Today Greens
  (flax seed, spirulina, and probiotics)

- 1 scoop of All-in-One Superfood (by Radiance Platinum)

- 1 cup of frozen antioxidant fruit (organic berries)

- 1 tsp of organic chia seeds

- ½ cup of gluten-free quick rolled oats

- 1 tsp of hemp seeds (organic or non-GMO

- 1 tsp of coconut oil (non-GMO)

- 1 tsp of honey

- 1 tbsp of goji berries or blueberries

- ¼ cup of almond milk (organic or non-GMO almond milk)

By following the above dietary plan and by eliminating thyroid toxic substances, Graves' disease can be controlled and thyroid levels can return back to normal.

Hyperemesis Gravidarum

Although there is no "cure" to treat hyperemesis gravidarum, there are certain vitamins and medications that can assist with the symptoms.

- Vitamins B6 and B12

- Ginger

- Zofran

- Reglan

- Intravenous fluids containing vitamin B6 and B12 if unable to be taken by mouth

- BRAT diet consisting of bananas, rice, apples, and toast

- Elimination of all strong orders and fragrances

- Pedialyte oral electrolyte solution

- Folic acid pills if prenatal pills are unable to be taken by mouth

My philosophy in life is to never give up hope. I believe in being my own advocate and researching as much as I can to have a happier and healthier way of life and to use natural remedies if I can. God designed each and every one of us, and He has something special planned for our lives. We must believe and know that He is with us every step of the way, through it all.

My advice at this age: listen to your body, listen to your gut, live life to the fullest each day, have no regrets, tell your families that you love them every day, do a good unselfish deed, take the time to sit outside for quiet moments, unplug from social media and electronics for a day, never put off till tomorrow what you can do today, be humble, be grateful, be thankful, and always know that God loves you and has a plan for your life.

CONCLUSION

The stories in this book cry out to women everywhere. Through their stories we traveled through years and the lives of homemakers, attorneys, hoteliers, writers, fitness gurus, philanthropists, and God.

The stories take you to the depths of despair where, as women, our hearts ache for others on difficult journeys, and how these women overcame or learned from their experiences.

These stories of women took you to a mother who had her children taken from her, and other women who couldn't or didn't have any children, but where their life's struggles and triumphs were in their own passage deep and different.

There were broken friendships, broken hearts, loneliness, and depression. We had divorce of parents that influenced them in their later years, including the movement of the ground under their feet far too often. We lost ourselves in the walk of life to sadness, men, and children . . . only to have found ourselves and who we really wanted to be, through these challenges.

We were sick, we lost weight and then gained weight, and we had an endless struggle with loving ourselves. We endured the death of loved ones, disease came upon many, which included breast cancer and mastectomies as well as some not so well-known conditions.

The women in these stories travel through perimenopause and menopause, and others are on the road to it. Regardless of the challenges, each and every day they try to claw ourselves out of whatever it was that had taken over our lives. For some we will learn about the aging body changes and how that causes us to look at the truth of age. It's such a shock to find out that our bodies have a mind of their own, certainly attached to our minds, but somehow a bit disconnected, and driving us to find out how we bring the body, mind, and spirit back together again. This happens through the process of understanding the pain and seeking the answer.

As we walked through the valley of the stories, we find ourselves. We find our hopes, anticipations, dreams, and solutions. You cannot help seeing in all of the journeys the desire to emerge and find the answer. Once found, it's like a gem to be discovered and shared. Once we travel through the darkest places and reach our heads above, we then can share all that we learned. You will find this in these women's stories, periods of time, or years that required endurance of spirit.

These stories remind us how pain can be our greatest teacher. If that's true for you, then you have found the right place to discover the turn-around. Gathered here are the joys and triumphs over difficult paths. As we embarked on our forties and fifties, the light came through the cracks and we came up through those cracks to inhale, realizing lungs full of air. We hope you, the reader, can see more than ever before and how as women we can support each other and be proud of each woman in this book, and the countless others who have their own truths to tell . . . each who walked the walk. In this book about some of our most difficult struggles, we all realized a truth in life where change is unavoidable.

To quote one of our writers in this book:

Listen to your body, listen to your gut, live life to the fullest each day, have no regrets, tell your families that you love them every day, do a good unselfish deed, take the time to sit outside for quiet moments, unplug from social media and electronics for a day, never put off till tomorrow what you can do today, be humble, be grateful, be thankful . . . .

And from the Dalai Lama,

It is worth remembering that the time of greatest gain in terms of wisdom and inner strength is often that of greatest difficulty.

Thank you for joining us on these journeys.

Andrea Lambert